Academic Word List

in Use

A self-study reference and practice book with answers

IELTSedits

Academic Word List

in Use

A self-study reference and practice book with answers

IELTSedits

ISBN: 978-0-9933668-1-9

For further information e-mail the IELTSedits team at:

enquiries@ieltsedits.com

The IELTSedits Team

The IELTSedits team - the authors of Academic Word List in Use - is also able to help IELTS students wanting to further improve not only their vocabulary. but other IELTS exam skills.

IELTS Writing

As one of the more difficult IELTS skills to master, it takes time to develop the experience needed to get grade 7.0 and above in writing.

However, IELTSedits offers you the chance to help your writing skills improve more quickly.

With over 50 years of combined experience (including IELTS examining) the IELTSedits team offers you the chance to really learn how to write IELTS tasks the way the examiner wants to see them.

We not only offer lots of writing tips but we can also suggest ways for you to improve by sending you a Student Report for every writing task you write.

For more information come and visit our website at - http://ieltsedits.com

Or write to the IELTSedits team at - enquiries@ieltsedits.com

The most frequently used words

The 1st 1,000 and 2nd 1,000 word frequency lists provided in Academic Word List in Use are known as the General Service List of English Words (GSL).

The GSL has been used as a basis for many series of graded readers, and this provides an advantage in using it as general study material. The lists used here were provided by the School of Linguistics and Applied Language Studies (LALS) at Victoria University of Wellington, New Zealand.

The Academic Word List (AWL) was developed and evaluated by Averil Coxhead at Victoria University for her MA thesis.

The GSL actually fall slightly short of 1,000 words per list with the 1st 1,000 words being 927 words and the 2nd 1,000 words being 978. This is the result of amendments over the years.

Contents

What universities think about the Academic Word List

This is a very important specialised vocabulary for learners intending to pursue academic studies in English at the secondary and post-secondary levels.
Kinsella San Francisco State University - USA

Based on meticulously-designed research carried out on the Academic Word List using an academic corpus of 3.5 million running words and 28 major disciplines, researchers have identified 10 sublists of academic words.
University of Toronto - Canada

The Academic Word List contains 570 of the most important words you need to know to be successful in your studies.
RMIT University - Melbourne - Australia

The 570 words in the Academic Word List are valuable for all students preparing for academic study, whether they are planning to follow a course in Medicine, Computer Systems Engineering, Architecture or European Law. If you are planning to continue your studies in English, this list will help you.
Nottingham University - United Kingdom

Having a strong active vocabulary is an important part of being able to achieve academic success.
Georgia State University - USA

These words are common in academic texts, but they are not so common in everyday writing or speech. This is why they are not so easy to learn, but why at the same time, it is very important for students to learn them. If you do not know these words, you will find academic work at university difficult.
University of Plymouth - United Kingdom

Introduction

You will need to know the Academic Word List (AWL) if you hope to study in an English-speaking university environment. In fact, because many of these words are very common, they are even useful to people who do not have academic goals of this kind.

Many of these words are frequently encountered in newspapers, magazines, and novels, and can be heard on television, radio, and movies or in everyday conversation. Exposure to all of these media helps you to learn these AWL words.

The following words are examples of the vocabulary contained within the AWL. You can see that the vocabulary ranges from everyday language to words of a more academic nature.

area	issue	capacity	qualitative	function	intrinsic
energy	similar	vary	hierarchy	environment	equate

Increase your academic comprehension by 10%
It has been found that if students know the 2,000 most commonly used words, 80% to 95% of a text can be understood depending on what type of text it is. The 570 word families of the AWL will provide an additional 4% comprehension of newspapers and 8.5% to 10% of academic text. If instead of learning the AWL, however, the student studies the 3rd 1,000 most frequent words, understanding will only increase by 4.3%.

10 Sublists
The Academic Word List in Use makes learning each word much easier than when learning from a typical vocabulary list because when you look at each new word you will also see how it can be used in a sentence.

Start with Sublist 1 which contains the most common words in the AWL. When these words become familiar to you, move on to Sublist 2 (the next most common words) and work all the way down to Sublist 10.

Review with gap fill exercises
You also have a chance to review each sublist with gap fill exercises at the end of each sublist and a final review at the end. Answers are at the end of the book.

Check each sublist for words you find in any text you read If the words are in the AWL, you should learn them. If they are not in the list, then check the 2,000 most frequent words. If the words are not in the most frequent 2000 words of English or the AWL, then think carefully about whether or not you need to learn them. You can look at the 2,000 most frequently used words on pages 71 to 82.

How to learn new words
Focus on really understanding these words rather than just recognising the words every time you see them. Do you REALLY know how to use each of these words in a sentence?

Word cards
Using word cards is one way of strengthening the connection between a word and how to use it. You can put a word on one side and the definition and a sentence with it in on the other. Test yourself from time to time.

i   Look at the definition and see if you know the word and then read the sentence.

i   Look at the word and see if you know the meaning. Write a sentence using the word..

Remember: this is a situation where by learning less than 600 words you will increase your academic
comprehension by 10%. This is a fantastic reward for the effort you put into this.

Once remembered these words are yours forever

As you begin to become more familiar with more and more words it is important to try and use them as often as possible when practicing your writing and speaking skills.

Writing an office report, giving a presentation, writing an IELTS essay are all wonderful opportunities to incorporate some of the words that you have been learning. Doing this whenever an opportunity arises will help strengthen a solid link between more and more words and how you use them.

Another effective way of improving these word links is by reading a newspaper, a journal, an office report and so on. Students who read on a daily basis will usually have a much better vocabulary range than students who only read when they study. Even 10 minutes reading a day will help you improve.

570 words - plus

Almost all of the 570 words in the Academic Word List are headwords of word families. This means that most of the words found in the AWL can be found in other forms. This might be something as simple as a singular noun becoming plural - economy / economies - or a verb changing tense - undergo / undergone.

This can also mean that a word like - analyze - is the headword for a range of words such as - analysis, analyzes, analyzed, analyzing, analyst, analytic, analytical, and analytically.

Therefore, studying Academic Word List in Use will allow you the opportunity to increase your vocabulary range far beyond the 570 words that you learn in this book. An ability to be flexible when reading will quickly help you to add more words to those that you know already.

You might find that some of the answers in the exercises on pages 3 - 6 and the Final Review section on pages 65 - 68 are forms of the headwords found in this book.

Academic Word List in Practice

To see how not knowing the AWL can affect your comprehension when reading, you are going to have the chance to look at a selection of reading passages taken from the New Scientist magazine.

Each reading passage is about 200 words in length and is an extract from a larger article. When you see each reading passage the AWL vocabulary will be missing For example, in an article titled - Animal brains connected up to make mind melded computers - you can see the passage like this:

Two heads are better than one and three monkey brains can control an avatar better than any single monkey. For the first time, a 1. _____has 2. _____the brains of multiple animals to form a living 3. _____ that can perform 4. _____ and solve problems.

If human brains could be 5. _____ connected, it might give us superhuman problem solving abilities and allow us to 6. _____ 7. _____thoughts and experiences. "It is really exciting," says Iyad Rahwan at the Masdar 8. _____in Abu Dhabi, UAE, who was not 9. _____in the work. "It will change the way humans 10. _____."

The work, 11. _today, is an advance on standard brain machine interfaces - 12. _____ that have 13. _____people and animals to control machines and prosthetic limbs by thought alone. These tend to work by 14. _____the brain's electrical activity into signals that a 15. _____can 16. _____.

Miguel Nicolelis at Duke University 17. _____Center in Durham, North Carolina and his 18. _____wanted to extend the idea by 19. _____multiple brains at once. The 20. _____ connected the brains of three monkeys to a 21. _____that controlled an animated screen 22. _____ representing a robotic arm, placing electrodes into brain 23. _____ 24. _____in movement.

Frequency of Words

The influence of the 1st 1,000 words, the 2nd 1,000 words and the AWL are shown as a percentage of the total number of words in the passage.

1st 1,000 words	66.67%
2nd 1,000 words	12.31%
Academic Word List	12.31%
Off List Words	8.72%

AWL – missing words

abstract - areas - co-operate - colleagues - communicate - computer (3x) - converting - devices enabled - image - incorporating - institute - interpret - involved (2x) - medical - networked published - similarly - tasks - team (2x)

(NOTE: The underlined words in the text are off list words and neither in the first 2,000 words or the Academic Word List and might be more specific vocabulary related to the topic.)

The answers are on page 69 if you want to try and complete the text.

New Scientist Text

Burst of light speeds up healing by turbocharging our cells

1st 1,000 words	73.54%
2nd 1,000 words	5.82%
Academic Word List	8,47%
Off List Words	12.17%

It sounds too good to be true. Shining red light on skin or cells in a dish gives an instant 1. _____ boost that could help heal wounds, relieve pain and perhaps help male infertility and other 2. _____ conditions.

The curious healing effect has been known for 3. _____ – 4. _____ have been 5. _____ its use in eye 6. _____ since 2002 – but why it works has been a mystery. It turns out the explanation could be simple and yet strange: the red light seems to 7. _____ the 8. _____ properties of water, which turbocharges the 9. _____ 10. _____that provide a cell's 11. _____.

The 12. _____has come from work led by Andrei Sommer of the University of Ulm in Germany.

The effect on cells of near-infrared light, which has a wavelength of 670 nanometres, was first reported 40 years ago. The light causes mitochondria, the cell's powerhouses, to produce more ATP, a 13. _____ that provides the cell's 14. _____.

Until now, the best explanation was that an important respiration enzyme called cytochrome C is 15. _____by the near-infrared 16. _____, but we now know that it doesn't absorb light at quite the right frequency.

AWL – missing words
affected - alter - chemical - compound - decades - energy (4x) - injuries - investigating - medical physical - reactions - researchers - revelation

The answers are on page 69 if you want to try and complete the text.

4

New Scientist Text

Spy tech firm breach exposes extent of world surveillance market

1st 1,000 words	64.80%
2nd 1,000 words	6.63%
Academic Word List	11.22%
Off List Words	17.35%

The hunters become the hunted. Yesterday, hackers 1. _____what they claimed was 400 GB of 2. _____ 3. _____stolen from Hacking 4. _____an Italian company that sells surveillance tools to governments and 5. _____agencies.

Ever since, 6. _____ 7. _____have been poring over the 8. _____and 9. _____their findings. For one thing, the 10. _____suggest Hacking 11. _____marketed its products to a wide 12. _____of governments – including a host of repressive 13. _____.

Christopher Soghoian, 14. _____technologist at the American 15. _____Liberties Union (ACLU), says he has downloaded a cache of company invoices in an effort to better understand which governments Hacking 16. _____sold its products to.

"The invoices are fascinating," he says. "Hacking 17. _____has been selling their software to governments like Azerbaijan and Kazakhstan, Sudan, Vietnam, Ethiopia – a number of governments with 18. _____histories of abusing human rights."

Soghoian admits that it's possible the leaked 19. _____have been tampered with in some way, but says his gut feeling is that they are largely authentic. "20. _____have been studying Hacking 21. _____for three or four years and the invoices match up with the countries we believe have been 22. _____this stuff in the first place," he says.

AWL – missing words
civil - documented - documents (3x) - experts - files - intelligence - internal - principal publishing - purchasing - range - regimes - released - researchers - security - team (5x)

The answers are on page 69 if you want to try and complete the text.

New Scientist Text

Winning formula reveals if your team is too far ahead to lose

1st 1,000 words	73.77%
2nd 1,000 words	7.10%
Academic Word List	9.29%
Off List Words	9.84%

After 1. _____ more than a million 2. _____ in basketball, hockey and American football – sports where contests have a fixed 3. _____ – Aaron Clauset of the University of Colorado, Boulder, and his 4. _____ have developed a way to help you decide.

Their 5. _____ set 6. _____ that much of the 7. _____ of these competitive 8. _____ sports can be 9. _____ captured by a simple model in which the score difference 10. _____ moves up or down over time. "It's kind of remarkable," said Clauset. "The 11. _____ behaviour of these highly trained athletes in a well 12. _____ 13. _____ is basically 14. _____ to a 15. _____ number generator."

The 16. _____ used their model to work out the probability that a lead would be "safe" at any given time. For an NBA basketball game lasting 48 minutes, they calculated that a 17. _____ with a lead of 18 points when the match is halfway through will win 90 per cent of the time. To work out what size of basketball lead is 90 per cent safe in general, multiply the square root of the remaining seconds in the game by 0.4602.

AWL – missing words
accurately - analysing - colleagues - data - duration - dynamics - emergent - encounters
environment - equivalent - random - randomly - regulated - researchers - revealed - team (2x)

The answers are on page 69 if you want to try and complete the text.

Sublist 1

analyze • approach • area • assess • assume • authority • available • benefit • concept • consist • constitute context • contract • create • data • define • derive • distribute • economy • environment • establish estimate • evident • export • factor • finance • formula • function • identify • income • indicate • individual interpret • involve • issue • labour • legal • legislate • major • method • occur • percent • period • policy principle • proceed • process • require • research • respond • role • section • sector • significant • similar source • specific • structure • theory • vary

analyze
Use the warm-up time to analyze your opponent's strengths and weaknesses.

approach
The best approach to tackling this problem is to develop a better public transportation system as well as increase car and fuel prices.

area
It might be more practical in today's competitive world if students develop more than one area of interest.

assess
It is important to assess the relative importance of each of these issues in order to decide which problem to work on first.

assume
Before getting upset, ask yourself what you can learn from the comment being made and assume good intentions from the speaker.

authority
Parents will be seen by their children as authority figures and as such should also be good role models and encourage good behaviour.

available
One advantage of studying overseas is that the colleges and universities are more likely to have a wider range of resources available than in your native country.

benefit
Each year in Britain, tens of thousands of families suffer in this way and would benefit from the protection that life insurance can offer.

concept
Happiness can be seen as a concept or state of mind that is very difficult to explain in simple terms.

consist
Anyone can do yoga, so classes consist of men and women and people of all ages.

constitute
In Denmark, where public servants constitute a special category of public employees, they have been denied the right to strike which is in violation of Article 6, paragraph 4.

context
A snide comment or remark made to a certain person can be taken out of context and may lead to long term disagreements.

contract
A contract is seen as a legal agreement between two parties.

create
Exercise can burn up the adrenalin that worry, fear and frustration create, leaving the body relaxed and rested.

data
After typing the article, one must save the file immediately to avoid loss of any unsaved data.

define
For years, astronomers tried to define a planet by shape, orbit around a star and its influence on other bodies.

derive
The pleasure we derive from journeys is perhaps dependent more on the mindset with which we travel than on the destination we travel to.

distribute
The landowner, on his retirement, decided to equally distribute a parcel of land to the deserving farmers as a reward for their hard work and dedication over many years.

economy
The economy of a country under crisis is mainly victim to high inflation and prevailing unemployment rates.

environment
Everyone must take part in the preservation of the environment if future generations are to inherit a world worth living on.

establish
A primary concern of a new business is to establish a network of connections and customers.

estimate
Did you know that you can create your own estimate of retirement benefits by using the Retirement Estimate Calculator on the TRS website?

evident
The teacher, with evident enjoyment, chastised the student for failing to submit his final paper on time.

export
Farmers are hoping for better infrastructure between the cities and more rural areas as this would enable them to bring their products to the cities where they could then export them.

factor
A successful career comes from three basic factors: knowledge about your chosen field, competency in the technical skills of your profession, and attitude towards your work and colleagues.

finance
There are a number of online platforms where investors sign up to find entrepreneurs looking for finance.

formula
The company's winning formula includes excellent service and quality products.

function
An independent auditor's primary function is to present the financial statements of a company.

identify
To know your capabilities as an employee, you must be able to identify your strengths and weaknesses and know what you can offer to the company.

income
It is often said that one must not spend more than ones' income if you intend to have a more secure future.

indicate
The police did not indicate in the report if it was a homicide or murder.

individual
Each individual has a role to play in society, reminding us to be role models for our future generation.

interpret
Dreams often interpret a real life situation that you have experienced or witnessed in some way.

involve
Chemical reactions always involve breaking and forming chemical bonds.

issue
The child labour issue involves about 217 million children working worldwide.

labour
A pregnant women can never predict with certainty when labour will begin, the due date given by the doctor is merely a point of reference.

legal
The employee was accused of harassing a co-worker and was subjected to the legal sanctions of the company.

legislate
Government officials everywhere feel the need to legislate for things they know little about and even less on how to deal with them effectively.

major
One of the major problems the country is facing is overpopulation. The government needs to address this problem immediately to avoid further overcrowding and congestion.

method
The natural family planning method is approved by the Roman Catholic Church as a means to avoid or postpone unwanted pregnancy.

occur
A midlife crisis might occur when you feel you are stuck in a career or other life situation that you can not escape from.

percent
The results of the board exam showed ninety nine percent of the reviewers passed the test with flying colours.

period
Mourning for the loss of a loved one takes an indefinite period of time before closure of this event can happen.

policy
The policy of the company is for every employee to be at the office sitting at their desk at least 10 minutes before 8am.

principle
The underlying principle of teamwork is for every team member to enjoy the camaraderie of working together and so develop mutual trust and friendship.

proceed
After every wedding, all guests are requested to proceed to the newlyweds' reception.

process
To process a driving license, one must complete a series of written and oral examinations.

require
Extraordinary claims require extraordinary evidence was a phrase made popular by Carl Sagan and is central to scientific method.

research
The salesman conducted research into selling used mobile phones to developing countries.

respond
In case of an emergency you may contact the number stated on the card and a registered member of the organization will respond immediately.

role
All parents should act responsibly because they serve as role models not just to their children but to others as well.

section
All legislation enacted under section 5 of the Fourteenth Amendment must be "congruent and proportional" to the unconstitutional harm it seeks to remedy.

sector
Certain respected individuals in the private sector support the governments' idea of privatizing the country's nuclear power plants.

significant
The president acknowledged that there have been significant problems with the application of the death penalty.

similar
The face of Mona Lisa has similar features to that of its creator, Leonardo da Vinci.

source
We all know that this organizations' main source of funding is through donations and pledges from various companies.

specific
Please be specific in choosing a colour for your motif so that we have enough time to print it before your upcoming event.

structure
The tallest freestanding structure in the world from 1975 -2007 was the CN Tower in Toronto, Canada.

theory
Please state in your own words possible flaws in the theory of evolution.

vary
Please note that the cost of each ticket may vary from time to time due to the availability of seats.

Gap Fill Exercises - Sublist 1

The exercises presented here give you an opportunity to review the words in Sublist 1.

Use the words from the box to complete the sentences below.

> area - assume - benefit - concept - contract
> environment - evident - finance - identify - income

1. Before getting upset, ask yourself what you can learn from the comment being made and _____ good intentions from the speaker

2. It is often said that one must not spend more than ones' _____ if you intend to have a more secure future.

3. There are a number of online platforms where investors sign up to find entrepreneurs looking for _____.

4. Each year in Britain, tens of thousands of families suffer in this way and would _____ from the protection that life insurance can offer.

5. To know your capabilities as an employee, you must be able to _____ your strengths and weaknesses and know what you can offer to the company.

6. A _____ is seen as a legal agreement between two parties.

7. It might be more practical in today's competitive world if students develop more than one _____ of interest.

8. Everyone must take part in the preservation of the _____ if future generations are to inherit a world worth living on.

9. Happiness can be seen as a _____ or state of mind that is very difficult to explain in simple terms.

10. The teacher, with _____ enjoyment, chastised the student for failing to submit his final paper on time.

Sublist 2

achieve • acquire • administrate • affect • appropriate • aspect • assist • category • chapter commission •community • complex • compute • conclude • conduct • consequent • construct • consume credit • culture • design • distinct • element • equate • evaluate • feature • final • focus • impact • injure institute • invest • item • journal • maintain • normal • obtain • participate • perceive • positive • potential previous • primary • purchase • range • region • regulate • relevant • reside • resource • restrict • secure seek • select • site • strategy • survey • text • tradition • transfer

achieve
To achieve your dreams, you must have the drive and passion to succeed and be willing to take risks.

acquire
Every child born of a married Dutch father or mother will automatically acquire Dutch nationality, even if he or she is born outside the Netherlands.

administrate
This course covers how administrators and project managers can set up and administrate one or several projects in the new software.

affect
The point of implementing policy through raising or lowering interest rates is to affect people's and firms' demand for goods and services.

appropriate
It is not appropriate for a lady to be seen coming home in the early hours of the morning.

aspect
Gaining good publicity for the school through establishing a high profile is an important aspect of marketing.

assist
For real progress to be made, we must realize that everyone must assist one another for the betterment of the country.

category
In New Orleans, the levees were designed for Category 3, but Katrina peaked at a Category 5 hurricane, with winds up to 175 mph.

chapter
For you to be able to move on with your life, you must try to close the chapter in your life where you experienced a lot of unhappiness and became rather bitter.

commission
The sales commission is a method of compensating salespeople for services they provide to their employer.

community
As a community, we are all obliged to follow the rules at all times.

complex
No matter how complex life maybe at times, there will always be a solution to all our problems. We just need to be strong and remember that these difficulties will pass.

compute
Our minds can't imagine a time span as long as a million years, let alone the thousands of millions of years that geologists routinely compute.

conclude
It took hours for the management to conclude that their concern over a security leak was a false alarm.

conduct
Government officials need to conduct research into how to boost the economy.

consequent
None of this alters the ethical issue and the consequent injustice done in 1985.

construct
The technical skill of the house martin enables it to construct gravity-defying mud nests beneath the eaves of houses.

consume
Vegetarians who consume eggs and milk should have no problem with obtaining enough vitamin B12.

credit
Children need to give due credit to their parents for the unconditional love they have received over the years.

culture
Alan Fountain was deeply involved in the independent film culture throughout the 1970's.

design
The project will assess existing courses on information seeking skills organised by the library and design new methods and materials for future courses.

distinct
The mastodon was even more distinct, since its teeth were unlike those of the modern elephants.

element
The young man had no clear idea on how to propose to his girlfriend but felt that an element of surprise on their anniversary would be ideal.

equate
His half-hearted apology does not equate to the pain she has been coping with because of the lies spread against her.

evaluate
The employees need to evaluate their own performance with honesty before being given a performance bonus for the quarter.

feature
O‡ feature '^ complementary medicine that patients may prefer is simply the longer consultations that its practitioners tend to give.

final
The decision made by the judge is considered final but if you feel the need to appeal, you must file a new case with the supreme court.

focus
We all need to focus more on our blessings rather than our misfortunes and struggles.

impact
Losing a job can create a huge impact on your life and may even lead to bankruptcy.

injure
Rampaging bulls gore three and injure eleven at the annual Running of the Bulls festival in Spain.

institute
The fashion institute offers all students a structured internship that is designed to help them in their chosen area of specialization.

invest
We will invest in the modernisation of our hospitals and tackle the backlog of repairs and maintenance.

item
The Australia Post delivery network has tracking capabilities, allowing you to view where your item is during the delivery process.

journal
Psychologists often suggest keeping a personal journal so that you can write down your daily insights.

maintain
The oil producers' organisation OPEC has decided to maintain current production levels despite calls from the industry to push oil prices higher.

normal
The store is now back to normal operations after the week long holiday.

obtain
You need to obtain a working visa if you intend to work abroad.

participate
Only about 70% of households approached agreed to participate in the Family Expenditure Survey.

perceive
The central concern for all these groups is with what they perceive to be declining moral standards.

positive
Sometimes we can find it difficult to visualise positive outcomes.

potential
Every potential candidate must follow a tedious process of panel interviews before making it to the top five and the final interview.

previous
In many cases the previous foreign owners of those companies which passed into local ownership were invited to continue as managers for which they received a management fee.

primary
Our teachers' primary concern is for their students to be able to grasp the subject being taught and for them to apply it in the real world.

purchase
Culture is generally regarded as a key determinant of consumer demand and purchase pattern.

range
Britain is geologically interesting because it contains many different rock formations containing a large range of metals.

region
The temperature in polar regions tends to be much colder during winter because they receive less intense solar radiation than the rest of the Earth.

regulate
The aim should be to develop your own potential, not to regulate your working habits to a conventional norm.

relevant
The personal lives of each employee is not a relevant part of a discussion when in a business meeting.

reside
To find out which office to contact, please select the country or territory where you legally reside.

resource

The closure of the company was mainly because of the very limited resources they had.

restrict

By then, the critical decision had been taken to restrict the flow of refugee children into Britain.

secure

Please ensure all your belongings are secure when in any crowded place in order to avoid any loss of your items.

seek

I would suggest that you seek help from a guidance counsellor to assess if you are emotionally and mentally burnt out.

select

Women tend to select their wardrobes from online stores because they don't have time to go to the malls.

site

The engineer needs to visit the site everyday so he can properly guide the workers.

strategy

The coach developed a great strategy for his team to follow and as a result they defeated their opponents in the finals.

survey

A recent survey showed that out of every ten university graduated women, six of them liked to relax in a bar after a hard day at work while four of them wanted to go home and have a good nights rest.

text

The boss received a text message from one of his employees asking for emergency leave approval because his son had been hospitalized.

tradition

It is a family tradition for many Asian people to celebrate New Year with their family.

transfer

Please transfer the patient to the operating room after he has finished his x-ray and other laboratory tests so that we can proceed with the operation.

Gap Fill Exercises - Sublist 2

The exercises presented here give you an opportunity to review the words in Sublist 2.

Use the words from the box to complete the sentences below.

administrate - affect - assist - chapter - equate
positive - potential - purchase - survey - tradition

1. A recent _____ showed that out of every ten university graduated women, six of them liked to relax in a bar after a hard day at work while four of them wanted to go home and have a good nights rest.

2. Sometimes we can find it difficult to visualise _____ outcomes.

3. For you to be able to move on with your life, you must try to close the _____in your life where you experienced a lot of unhappiness and became rather bitter.

4. Every _____candidate must follow a tedious process of panel interviews before making it to the top five and the final interview.

5. The point of implementing policy through raising or lowering interest rates is to _____ people's and firms' demand for goods and services.

6. Culture is generally regarded as a key determinant of consumer demand and _____ pattern.

7. It is a family _____ for many Asian people to celebrate New Year with their family.

8. This course covers how administrators and project managers can set up and _____one or several projects in the new software.

9. His half-hearted apology does not _____to the pain she has been coping with because of the lies spread against her.

10. For real progress to be made, we must realize that everyone must _____one another for the betterment of the country.

Sublist 3

alternative • circumstance • comment • compensate • component • consent • considerable • constant constrain • contribute • convene • coordinate • core • corporate • correspond • criteria • deduce demonstrate • document • dominate • emphasis • ensure • exclude • framework • fund • illustrate immigrate • imply • initial • instance • interact • justify • layer • link • locate • maximize • minor negate • outcome • partner • philosophy • physical • proportion • publish • react • register • rely remove • scheme • sequence • sex • shift • specify • sufficient • task • technical • technique technology • valid • volume

alternative
Herbal medicine has stood the test of time and has proven itself to be a good alternative to allopathic medicine.

circumstance
Therefore, the experience of women will vary systematically over time, place and circumstance, in step with, but different from, the experience of men.

comment
Scotland Yard refused to comment on whether they believed the IRA were responsible.

compensate
Deaf dogs can manage surprisingly well, with their eyesight and sense of smell helping to compensate for their lack of hearing.

component
An important component of physical fitness is cardiovascular endurance. It is the ability of the body to experience sustained exercise like jogging, running, cycling and swimming.

consent
You must obtain your parent's consent before you can join the summer camp.

considerable
Pregnancy causes considerable challenges for mothers-to-be like morning sickness, heartburn, and leg cramps.

constant
Karate has quite a high drop-out rate because of the hard work involved and the constant repetition of techniques.

constrain
The study will examine the factors and forces which promote and constrain local economic growth.

contribute
Every person in Canada 18 years of age and older, who works and who earns more than $3,500 per year must contribute to the Canada Pension Plan.

19

convene
The Secretary of State for the Environment will convene a new private sector forum to promote London internationally as a business, tourist and cultural centre.

coordinate
The need to coordinate regularly with your family as to your whereabouts when travelling in other countries is essential.

core
Every new employee must go through a series of training programs to familiarize themselves with the company's core values.

corporate
Through such corporate crimes as bribing foreign and domestic governmental officials, and price-fixing, some competing corporations are forced into bankruptcy.

correspond
She must respect the ideas and methods of the hospital ward, provided of course that these correspond to accepted hospital practice.

criteria
Over the years I have developed a profound belief that the Foreign Office has criteria entirely its own.

deduce
If a dog is man's best friend, it seems logical to deduce that he will stay loyal to his master at all times.

demonstrate
You need to demonstrate how to use the new photocopy machine as it is quite different to the previous one.

document
The student submitted all the pertinent documents when he applied for a scholarship to one of the most prestigious universities in the U.S.

dominate
Two opposing views continue to dominate the discussions about when children should start to learn a foreign language.

emphasis
The story's message gives emphasis to how children should give respect to their parents and teachers.

ensure
We need to ensure that the document was sent and if so whether or not it has already been received by our customer.

exclude
The benefits are intended for every citizen and should not, therefore, exclude senior citizens from availing from such privileges.

framework
The conceptual framework of the project is to highlight the need for a more efficient rapid transport system in the country.

fund
Before funds can be released, there is a need for proper documentation and approval from the City Treasurer's office.

illustrate
The following examples clearly illustrate some of the possible solutions to this serious problem.

immigrate
Many families want to immigrate to other countries to have a better future with more chances of getting jobs with bigger salaries.

imply
This does not imply that the individual has no role to play in resolving some of these issues.

initial
The initial process in applying for a student visa takes about one week.

instance
For an instance, when I stepped out of my comfort zone, I began to realize that there is a whole world waiting for me if I dare to take risks.

interact
It is difficult to say conclusively that there are differences in the way in which teachers in the classroom interact with Afro-Caribbean pupils.

justify
The statistics justify the claim that prison is being used in a strategic way against asylum seekers.

layer
The thick layers of clothing she wore saved her from the bitterly cold winter.

link
The link between mother and child is a special bond that no one can ever separate.

locate
Please locate these items in the warehouse so we can ship them immediately to our customer.

maximize
Students are helped to maximize their performance, to cope with academic and other difficulties that may arise and to prepare for the future beyond the course.

minor
She has only recently returned to full duties, and was treated for shock and minor cuts.

negate
Researchers have discovered some natural ways to negate the spread of cancer throughout the body.

outcome
It is impossible to predict the real outcome of such measures but it is clear that if nothing is done then these environmental problems will get worse.

partner
To have a successful business, you and your business partner must have the same passion and drive to succeed.

philosophy
He blamed the decline in sales on 'the erosion of distribution channels' and on management philosophy, which 'must clearly undergo a radical change'.

physical
For some reason, mental illness that produces physical symptoms is relegated to the status of an 'imaginary' disease.

proportion
They say that the quality of a persons' life is in direct proportion to their drive for continued excellence.

publish
With branch offices worldwide, we publish more than 600 books and 130 journals a year in the diverse fields of science, technology, medicine and business management.

react
Do not react immediately to every negative comment but instead try to use it as a positive lesson for you to keep on improving.

register
All citizens 18 years old and above must register by the end of the month to be able to vote in this upcoming election.

rely
Whereas 70 per cent of working women rely on relatives to provide childcare support, this option is often unavailable to professional women working full-time in demanding jobs.

remove
A Ryanair flight was forced to do a u-turn just 20 minutes after departure after the crew realised that they had forgotten to remove luggage from a previous flight.

scheme
It's true that a pale colour palette can make a small space appear larger, but a dark colour scheme can add drama.

sequence
Support for this sequence of events has come from animal models of atherosclerosis and studies using cell-culture techniques.

sex
The government has been quite apprehensive in approving same sex marriages.

shift
As its name implies, this is a shift in the atomic energy levels from one isotope of a particular element to the next.

specify
Many job advertisements specify the particular qualifications needed to apply.

sufficient
If you are losing weight, then you are not consuming sufficient calories daily.

task
In the late 1960s it rightly concluded that none of the artificial hearts available were fit for the task for which they had been designed.

technical
Nor is it a question of quality; our technical standards are higher, our news programmes better illustrated, and our interviewers more competent, than in any other country.

technique
The most effective technique in dealing with a difficult customer is to treat them with utmost respect and always explain things to them in a manner they can fully understand.

technology
It was the Judaeo-Christian work ethic which produced the Industrial Revolution and brought modern technology to the West.

valid
He recognised that valid points were being made by both sides.

volume
The volume of inquiries increased significantly after they posted their advertisement in the newspaper.

Gap Fill Exercises - Sublist 3

The exercises presented here give you an opportunity to review the words in Sublist 3.

Use the words from the box to complete the sentences below.

> alternative - circumstance - compensate - consent
> funds - link - layers - maximise - partner - technique

1. To have a successful business, you and your business _____must have the same passion and drive to succeed.

2. Students are helped to _____their performance, to cope with academic and other difficulties that may arise and to prepare for the future beyond the course.

3. The most effective _____in dealing with a difficult customer is to treat them with utmost respect and always explain things to them in a manner they can fully understand.

4. Therefore, the experience of women will vary systematically over time, place and _____, in step with, but different from, the experience of men.

5. Deaf dogs can manage surprisingly well, with their eyesight and sense of smell helping to _____for their lack of hearing.

6. The _____between mother and child is a special bond that no one can ever separate.

7. The thick _____of clothing she wore saved her from the bitterly cold winter.

8. Herbal medicine has stood the test of time and has proven itself to be a good _____to allopathic medicine.

9. You must obtain your parent's _____before you can join the summer camp.

10. Before _____can be released, there is a need for proper documentation and approval from the City Treasurer's office.

Sublist 4

access • adequate • annual • apparent • approximate • attitude • attribute • civil • code • commit
communicate • concentrate • confer • contrast • cycle • debate • despite • dimension • domestic • emerge
error • ethnic • goal • grant • hence • hypothesis • implement • implicate • impose • integrate • internal
investigate • job • label • mechanism • obvious • occupy • option • output • overall • parallel • parameter
phase • predict • principal • prior • professional • project • promote • regime • resolve • retain • series
statistic • status • stress • subsequent • sum • summary • undertake

access
The fastest, simplest, most reliable remote access to your computer from anywhere.

adequate
The human right to adequate housing is the right of every woman, man, youth and child to gain and sustain a safe and secure home and community in which to live in peace and dignity.

annual
The annual thanksgiving party is cancelled due to the new cost cutting measures.

apparent
There is no apparent reason why he left the country without telling us where he was going.

approximate
The growth axis was said to approximate the product life-cycle, with the rate of growth slowing down as the product market entered a more mature state.

attitude
Singapore is a famously good place to shop and eat, and recent shifts of attitude by both government and tourism chiefs have made it more interesting and attractive.

attribute
It has been recognised how difficult it is to attribute accurately the effect of humans on soil erosion because of many other crucial variables, such as climatic change.

civil
The couple lost everything in the savage civil war that has gripped their homeland.

code
In the Second World War, Alan Turing was the most important figure in the breaking of the German Enigma code.

commit
Stars in show business are twice as likely as other people to die in accidents and three times as likely to commit suicide, according to an American researcher.

communicate
Lilly believes that humans and dolphins can communicate with each other despite their physical differences.

concentrate
The most important area on which to concentrate was the massive amount of water required by the production of textiles.

confer
The Gulf War has demonstrated that the mere accumulation of data doesn't confer an automatic advantage unless it is complemented by quality analysis and contextual detail.

contrast
Working-class children, by contrast, are often raised by a female relative in the country - usually a grandmother or an aunt.

cycle
Yotel, a hotel chain that largely operates in airports around the world, operates a cycle to work scheme for their staff to further reduce their carbon footprint and keep their team fighting fit!

debate
Over the years since then, the debate on whether it was better to cross the English Channel by tunnel, bridge or ferry had raged to and fro.

despite
Despite the spread of private pensions, 75% of pensioners lived on less than £3,500 a year.

dimension
The incident assumed a diplomatic dimension when seven of the demonstrators sought refuge in the newly opened Papua New Guinea consulate.

domestic
Where the roles have been strictly divided, a man may feel like a stranger in his own house, lacking the domestic experience to share the chores.

emerge
Further evidence continued to emerge during the second half of 1989 that the world was becoming gradually warmer.

error
When you report the results of a statistical survey, you need to include the margin of error.

ethnic
A report published by the Commission for Racial Equality in 1987 also suggested that British trained doctors from ethnic minorities had trouble in getting the best jobs.

goal
Our goal is to make this world a better place to live in by constructing houses that are made from recycled material and use solar power.

grant
Lots of young people have to work in their summer holidays in order to supplement a meagre college grant.

hence
It has almost no taste at all, hence its use as a bulking agent in the food industry.

hypothesis
A hypothesis can be seen as an 'educated guess' based on prior knowledge and observation.

implement
Some of these ideas might be very expensive to implement and others take a long time to see results but the government must take immediate steps to help solve these problems.

implicate
The study is one of the first to implicate global warming from human activities as one of the factors that played into the Syrian conflict.

impose
We shall impose a penalty for those not able to settle their dues by the date shown in the contract.

integrate
Culture and religion also serve to integrate the immigrant community and to insulate it from a wider society.

internal
When such children become adults they suffer considerable internal conflict.

investigate
A study to investigate similar effects for the right hemisphere was originally considered as part of this work, but was abandoned due to lack of availability of subjects.

job
Training is based on six years of relevant job experience and an average two years' study.

label
I only intended to do that first album, because it was a new label and I didn't want to sign to a label that had no track record.

mechanism
All the common symptoms of a panic attack can thus be understood in terms of adrenalin being pumped round the body and in terms of the fight/flight mechanism.

obvious
Looking at it from a businessman's point of view, it's the obvious thing to do.

occupy
Please do not occupy the front seats as they are intended for the VIP visitors.

option
Going to university straight after graduating from high school isn't your only option as many students prefer to have a gap year first.

output
Firms reacted to the expansion of demand by raising prices, as well as expanding output, in order to try and raise profit margins.

overall
Overall, the sense was that women were subordinate to the masculine culture of work but were central to the world of the family.

parallel
In scores of other towns, on the other hand, the market places have been partly built over, so that one gets a broad main street, a block of buildings down one side and behind that again a narrow street running parallel to the main street.

parameter
A population parameter is a constant value that does not change, whereas a statistic will vary depending on the sample from which it was calculated.

phase
There will be two or three years work before this phase is complete.

predict
The model behaves so much like the real thing that the Berkeley scientists believe they can predict what would happen to the building during an earthquake.

principal
The value of one of the principal recommendations, the provision of psychiatric care to attempted suicide patients, remains controversial.

prior
The roses were placed in water prior to being pressed gradually as the petals opened.

professional
A special advantage is the involvement of university staff and students with a professional interest in child development.

project
Television news personnel feel duty-bound, in times of social and political crisis, to project a pro-establishment view of industrial conflict.

promote
The officials want to promote innovation in traditional industries, such as steelmaking and clothing, to the tune of £210 million over four years.

regime
They also pressed for a purge of supporters of the former communist regime on the university campuses and for increased student participation in university faculty councils.

resolve
The ability of any government to resolve these crises would depend on their ability to raise revenue and mobilise public support.

retain
If rural areas are to absorb and retain more labour than they have been expected to do in the past then agriculture and other forms of primary production will have a key role to play.

series
That's because the series of eruptions that killed 350 people in June 1992 left a 3,000-mile long cloud of ash and sulphur dioxide circling the earth.

statistic
More disturbing was this statistic: that while seven out of eight of those who died of lung cancer were heavy smokers, only one heavy smoker in eight died of lung cancer.

status
The Apple Watch is the nicest smart watch available, but critics might view it as more of a status symbol than a useful watch.

stress
There are numerous emotional and physical disorders that have been linked to stress including depression, heart attacks, certain cancers as well as rheumatoid arthritis.

subsequent
Subsequent research has documented that this effect occurs at the B- and T-cell levels.

sum
Your monthly payments are solely made up of interest: you do not repay a penny of the capital sum.

summary
Inevitably, this brief summary of a major debate surrounding change and continuity in British politics ignores a whole range of issues.

undertake
Students who do not undertake the period of industrial placement complete the degree in three years.

Gap Fill Exercises - Sublist 4

The exercises presented here give you an opportunity to review the words in Sublist 4.

Use the words from the box to complete the sentences below.

> adequate - debate - emerge - error - investigate
> obvious - option - parallel - project - regime

1. Television news personnel feel duty-bound, in times of social and political crisis, to _____ a pro-establishment view of industrial conflict.

2. A study to _____ similar effects for the right hemisphere was originally considered as part of this work, but was abandoned due to lack of availability of subjects.

3. In scores of other towns, on the other hand, the market places have been partly built over, so that one gets a broad main street, a block of buildings down one side and behind that again a narrow street running _____ to the main street.

4. The human right to _____ housing is the right of every woman, man, youth and child to gain and sustain a safe and secure home and community in which to live in peace and dignity.

5. Over the years since then, the _____ on whether it was better to cross the English Channel by tunnel, bridge or ferry had raged to and fro.

6. They also pressed for a purge of supporters of the former communist _____ on the university campuses and for increased student participation in university faculty councils.

7. When you report the results of a statistical survey, you need to include the margin of _____.

8. Going to university straight after graduating from high school isn't your only _____ as many students prefer to have a gap year first.

9. Looking at it from a businessman's point of view, it's the _____ thing to do.

10. Further evidence continued to _____ during the second half of 1989 that the world was becoming gradually warmer.

Sublist 5

academy • adjust • alter • amend • aware • capacity • challenge • clause • compound • conflict • consult
contact • decline • discrete • draft • enable • energy • enforce • entity • equivalent • evolve • expand
expose • external • facilitate • fundamental • generate • generation • image • liberal • license • logic
margin • medical • mental • modify • monitor • network • notion • objective • orient • perspective
precise • prime • psychology • pursue • ratio • reject • revenue • stable • style • substitute • sustain
symbol • target • transit • trend • version • welfare • whereas

academy
Zeisl, who was born in Vienna, showed early determination to compose, and entered the
Vienna State Academy of Music at the age of fourteen.

adjust
The most difficult aspect of a merger is trying to put a team together of people who come
from different business cultures and trying to adjust them to a different end.

alter
We now know this threatens to dramatically alter the world's weather patterns, raising sea
levels and bringing floods, droughts and famines to us and the Third World.

amend
The Government will amend the law relating to the employment rights of pregnant women.

aware
You should, as the potential employee, be well aware of the market pay and what you are
willing to be paid to perform the job that you're applying for.

capacity
Two thousand more workers are expected to be taken on and the local economy should get
a £100 million boost once production reaches capacity.

challenge
The challenge - more urgent now than it was even in the cold war - is to think differently
and to act otherwise.

clause
The buyer will find it difficult to argue that the clause was not agreed upon if it is contained
in a document signed by him.

compound
Prisoners' lack of contact with the outside world compound their problems.

conflict
This is one of a number of things which have brought English winemakers into conflict
with the European Community.

consult
If what you see or have seen is at variance with what is set down in the documents, then it is vital that you consult your solicitor before exchanging contracts.

contact
Police have appealed for anyone in the area who may have seen people acting suspiciously near the bank to contact them immediately.

decline
The decline of infant mortality makes it easier to accept the idea of smaller family size.

discrete
Similarly, managers in nearly every industry have learned from Japanese firms to look at quality control and inventory management as continuous processes, rather than discrete tasks.

draft
Any new government which does not want to be caught out should draft the necessary statute changes as a priority.

enable
Most of those whom the king preserved in office were men of the middle nobility, men whose experience would enable them to take effective charge of those placed under them.

energy
The sceptics at General Motors reckoned it could never work - the motor would overheat and no battery could store enough energy to turn over a car's engine.

enforce
More covert reasons may also underlie the inability (or reticence) of government forest agencies in developing countries to enforce regulations.

entity
They want Europe to become one entity and they will rapidly reject the national frontiers of the European member countries, which are now losing their residual relevance.

equivalent
The agency allowed the companies to continue selling their generic drugs, but gave them six months to either prove the drugs were equivalent, or remove them from the market.

evolve
Archaeology has become significantly more scientific, with the result that science is helping it evolve from being something of a treasure hunt to a high tech study.

expand
He was a major beneficiary of the video boom and used his profits to diversify and expand abroad.

expose

Friends of the Earth (FoE) have announced their 1991 "Green Con" awards, designed to expose organizations making spurious environmental claims.

external

The international businessman is battered and buffeted by so many external forces that even if he is operating skilfully within his own limitations he may not always win.

facilitate

It has been suggested that smoking causes a local immunological defect, which could facilitate the infection and persistence of human papillomavirus.

fundamental

The fundamental concept of sharing is giving without thinking of getting something in return.

generate

Media reports of torture often generate widespread public outrage.

generation

This in turn was involved with government policies for promoting the nuclear generation of electricity, open cast mining and the privatization of electricity generation, with the threatened increased use of cheap imported coal.

image

'We dropped the name (and image) because it gave the wrong impression by sounding like an extension of an army camp,' says a Raleigh International spokeswoman.

liberal

Since 1945, West Germany has become a 'normal' liberal democracy, with close affinities to the political systems of other western countries.

license

The two are negotiating to resolve the dispute, but if they fail to reach agreement, Microsoft would have to develop its own technology for linking Windows clients to NetWare or license similar code from a third party.

logic

She kept repeating to herself that it was an irrational fear, but logic did nothing to quell the lurking terror.

margin

Do companies realise that incidents, which are usually preventable, may be costing 10 per cent or more of their operating margin?

medical

To request your medical record, send a written request with your medical record number, full name at the time of treatment and your signature.

mental
The regular use of drugs can lead to a mental and physical craving for them.

modify
In summary, animals can modify their behaviour as a consequence of their experiences.

monitor
In order to monitor the implementation of the action project plans, a variety of data collection sources were used.

network
The long-term aim is to develop a network of groups and individuals who are prepared to speak out for democratic rights.

notion
Nevertheless, the notion that every new advance in education can be made by utilising existing resources more effectively is simplistic and does not bear close scrutiny.

objective
The objective is to provide the student with a basic knowledge of normal human biology with aspects relevant to clinical medicine.

orient
Networking is about helping other people and to do this you have to orient yourself toward thinking of other people before thinking of yourself.

perspective
An interesting perspective on the nature of the problem can be given by a graph plotting the number of dispersals against the date of publication of the books disposed of.

precise
Enzymes are a form of protein made out of a very precise order of amino acids.

prime
The world - and especially the empirical (the sensate) world - is becoming the prime focus of attention.

psychology
Contemporary psychology has come a long way from the time when J. B. Watson, the first behaviourist, forbade the consideration of non-observable entities.

pursue
I had hoped you would be able to help me but since you say you can't I shall have to pursue other avenues.

ratio
Stock turnover, as well as capital turnover, is an important ratio, reflecting both profitability and liquidity, as does the ratio of sales to debtors.

reject
People often reject creative ideas even when espousing creativity as a desired goal.

revenue
In business, revenue or turnover is income that a company receives from its normal business activities, usually from the sale of goods and services to customers.

stable
Advantages of the ancient method of water transportation include a stable water-flow with little vaporisation and energy consumption that is almost negligible.

style
By understanding the behavioural styles of others you can adapt the way in which you communicate to your employees to meet their needs and get the results you want.

substitute
An interesting and ambitious solution to the oil import bill problem is to substitute synthetic petrol made from natural gas.

sustain
In a desertifying world short of water, the utilitarian camel, and the ancient cultures that depend on it, offer a way to use land too poor to sustain anything else.

symbol
Throughout Napoleon's exile the violet had been the symbol of the Bonapartistes for the violet was the flower which, like the deposed Emperor, would return in the spring.

target
Two-thirds of the homes have been constructed and the remainder are on target for an autumn completion.

transit
It is horrifying that anyone in transit can find their way on to an aircraft undetected.

trend
The general trend appears to have been towards making it more difficult for people to stay on in full-time employment after 65.

version
If you find malware in your free scan consider upgrading to our premium version.

welfare
The largest part of the current welfare budget is paid out on national insurance benefits - such as old-age pensions and unemployment pay.

whereas
Some people believe that schools are responsible for the behaviour of their students, whereas others argue that discipline is the responsibility of parents.

Gap Fill Exercises - Sublist 5

The exercises presented here give you an opportunity to review the words in Sublist 5.

Use the words from the box to complete the sentences below.

```
consult - expose - fundamental - generation - margin
pursue - sustain - reject - transit - whereas
```

1. If what you see or have seen is at variance with what is set down in the documents, then it is vital that you _____ your solicitor before exchanging contracts.

2. People often _____ creative ideas even when espousing creativity as a desired goal.

3. The _____ concept of sharing is giving without thinking of getting something in return.

4. In a desertifying world short of water, the utilitarian camel, and the ancient cultures that depend on it, offer a way to use land too poor to _____ anything else.

5. I had hoped you would be able to help me but since you say you can't I shall have to _____ other avenues.

6. It is horrifying that anyone in _____ can find their way on to an aircraft undetected.

7. Friends of the Earth (FoE) have announced their 1991 "Green Con" awards, designed to _____ organizations making spurious environmental claims.

8. Some people believe that schools are responsible for the behaviour of their students, _____ others argue that discipline is the responsibility of parents.

9. This in turn was involved with government policies for promoting the nuclear generation of electricity, open cast mining and the privatization of electricity _____, with the threatened increased use of cheap imported coal.

10. Do companies realise that incidents, which are usually preventable, may be costing 10 per cent or more of their operating _____?

Sublist 6

abstract • accurate • acknowledge • aggregate • allocate • assign • attach • author • bond • brief • capable
cite • cooperate • discriminate • display • diverse • domain • edit • enhance • estate • exceed • expert
explicit • federal • fee • flexible • furthermore • gender • ignorant • incentive • incidence • incorporate
index • inhibit • initiate • input • instruct • intelligence • interval • lecture • migrate • minimum • ministry
motive • neutral • nevertheless • overseas • precede • presume • rational • recover • reveal • scope
subsidy • tape • trace • transform • transport • underlie • utilize

abstract
The most effective way of exploring this difficult question is not in abstract, unrealistic terms but in very practical ways.

accurate
In fact, a healthy skin is a reflection of good health in general; the skin is an accurate barometer of emotional and physical harmony and indeed, disharmony.

acknowledge
I should be grateful if you would acknowledge the receipt of this letter.

aggregate
Many of soccer's most important club competitions are played on a knockout basis with the winner decided by adding together the scores from the two games - the aggregate score.

allocate
In addition, they would allocate local grants and manage local parks and libraries.

assign
This FAQ contains instructions on how to assign Skype numbers to your members, reallocate Skype numbers and cancel Skype numbers assigned to your members.

attach
To attach a file to a message you're composing, follow the steps below.

author
Selecting the right publisher is one of the most important decisions an author will make.

bond
There is no stronger bond than the bond between siblings.

brief
Brief intervention is a technique used to initiate change for an unhealthy or risky behaviour such as smoking, lack of exercise or alcohol misuse.

capable
The world's first artificial leg capable of simulating the sensations of a real limb, even feeling pain, has been revealed by researchers at an Austrian university.

cite
Experts cite the same country as a possible future instance where human rights violations could lead to a call for action from outside national boundaries.

cooperate
No prison could run for long if not for the fact that most prisoners most of the time are prepared simply to cooperate with the staff and serve their time.

discriminate
At birth the baby's vision is blurred and cannot discriminate between foreground and background in the visual panorama.

display
Mother would not permit my brothers to slap my face or bottom, as she abhorred any display of violence.

diverse
As a manager rises in seniority, he will find it necessary to behave in a culturally diverse manner to satisfy the requirements of his job and the expectations of his employees.

domain
The majority of the digital copies featured are in the public domain or under an open license all over the world.

edit
While every effort will be made to publish contributions in full, the editor does reserve the right to edit the readers' letters when necessary.

enhance
Many of the flavourings which enhance our food today have not been thoroughly tested to ensure their safety.

estate
Cities naturally grew up next to the tracks and railway land thus became Canada's prime real estate.

exceed
An optimum time is set for the course, and penalties awarded if competitors exceed it.

expert
But as far as this security expert is concerned, unless Oxford University tightens up on security, and fast, more of its treasures will inevitably be stolen.

explicit
It is possible that firms could agree to co-ordinate their actions in some way without explicit communication and discussion.

federal
The actions of the Federal Reserve impact not just the US economy, and financial institutions, but individual investors and savers alike.

fee
Private patients can occupy separate accommodation and be treated by the specialist of their choice, in return for paying a fee.

flexible
More could be done to encourage flexible or staggered working hours and spread the traffic load.

furthermore
Furthermore, she also showed that the number of hours spent by women doing housework had actually risen between 1950 and 1971.

gender
Yet finding out what happens in higher education is of utmost importance in understanding the patterns of gender inequality that exist.

ignorant
Many of the workers there are either ignorant or careless about where they tip their waste.

incentive
The chance to study overseas will provide them with an incentive for continuing their education.

incidence
Uranium mines are known to have an increased incidence of lung cancer owing to exposure to radon, but only recently has the importance of radon in the home been acknowledged.

incorporate
Nor was Britain the only colonial power to incorporate existing native rulers into a system of colonial administration.

index
Table I shows the distribution of the women according to waist-hip ratio, body mass index, and age, and the percentage that became pregnant in each category.

inhibit
Dietary sulphate may allow growth of sulphate reducing bacteria which inhibit the growth of methanogenic bacteria.

initiate
The central government can sometimes initiate these rather more informal approaches towards economic and physical renewal.

input
One of my favourite things about my iPhone is how easy it is to configure the keyboard for Chinese input without installing any apps.

instruct
Because of the cost involved, it is rare for an investor to instruct its accountants or lawyers actually to proceed with this exercise until the main terms of the acquisition and investment have been agreed and the offer letter signed.

intelligence
Undoubtedly some will be unable to cope with this emphasis on self-management because they lack either the intelligence or perhaps, more importantly, the motivation to do so.

interval
The children were assessed on two occasions, each separated by a three-month interval.

lecture
Too many notes obscure the overall shape and conceal the essential content of a lecture.

migrate
There, men frequently migrate to the towns, leaving their families behind either to be visited at weekends or to join them in the town at a later date.

minimum
In Peru a worker with a minimum salary - already a privileged person - must work today seven times longer to earn the price of a kilo of rice than he did in 1981.

ministry
That declaration was issued on 27 September; by the end of October, a document was coming out of Croatia from the Ministry of Education and Culture.

motive
A hidden agenda is where someone's behaviour is determined by a motive which is undeclared and being deliberately concealed.

neutral
A neutral stance in relation to moral and spiritual development of pupils is not acceptable to the Catholic community especially in the Catholic school.

nevertheless
Nevertheless, it is an early maturing variety well suited to the long ripening period of a northern wine region.

overseas
Part of the problem is that much of this produce is exported and, therefore, land which could have been utilised to feed a domestic market is supplying an overseas population.

precede
Sometimes a tingling sensation in the arm will precede a heart attack.

40

presume
One may presume that the standard of living of both these groups was above the national average, thus giving them better resistance to disease than their poorer neighbours.

rational
One prevalent notion is that this self-improvement can be achieved through encouraging less rational, more intuitive, styles of thinking, and that dreams represent this ideal.

recover
Although the ultimate goal of rehabilitation is for the patient to be able to walk and function independently, not all patients can be expected to recover fully.

reveal
The songs are simplistic but still reveal an imaginative, sensitive mind at work.

scope
Companies with a narrow competitive scope may focus only on limited products, certain types of buyers, or specific geographical areas.

subsidy
No subway system in the world (save Hong Kong's) makes a profit; in Rome, 82 per cent of public transport operating costs are met by public subsidy, in Paris, 52 per cent.

tape
At the time of writing it seems that digital tape recorders sold to the public will have various anti-piracy measures built into them for this very reason.

trace
I've tried to trace the manufacturer, but I believe that they have ceased trading.

transform
We recommend three simple and proven techniques to transform your resume.

transport
With the unified Europe and excellent transport network now in place, the necessity for having a manufacturing plant in every country falls away.

underlie
I would like to consider some of the attitudes and concerns that underlie those issues.

utilize
Those of us who feel we are too busy or not dedicated enough to set aside time for exercise periods can utilize our daily routine to provide at least some opportunities to keep fit.

Gap Fill Exercises - Sublist 6

The exercises presented here give you an opportunity to review the words in Sublist 6.

Use the words from the box to complete the sentences below.

```
attach  - cooperate  - diverse  - enhance  - exceed
federal  - incentive  - incorporate - precede  - reveal
```

1. Nor was Britain the only colonial power to _____existing native rulers into a system of colonial administration.

2. Sometimes a tingling sensation in the arm will _____a heart attack.

3. To _____a file to a message you're composing, follow the steps below.

4. As a manager rises in seniority, he will find it necessary to behave in a culturally _____ manner to satisfy the requirements of his job and the expectations of his employees.

5. No prison could run for long if not for the fact that most prisoners most of the time are prepared simply to _____with the staff and serve their time.

6. The songs are simplistic but still _____an imaginative, sensitive mind at work.

7. The chance to study overseas will provide them with an _____for continuing their education.

8. An optimum time is set for the course, and penalties awarded if competitors _____it.

9. The actions of the _____Reserve impact not just the US economy, and financial institutions, but individual investors and savers alike.

10. Many of the flavourings which _____our food today have not been thoroughly tested to ensure their safety.

Sublist 7

adapt • adult • advocate • aid • channel • chemical • classic • comprehensive • comprise • confirm
contrary • convert • couple • decade • definite • deny • differentiate • dispose • dynamic • eliminate
empirical • equip • extract • file • finite • foundation • globe • grade • guarantee • hierarchy • identical
ideology • infer • innovate • insert • intervene • isolate • media • mode • paradigm • phenomenon
priority • prohibit • publication • quote • release • reverse • simulate • sole • somewhat • submit
successor • survive • thesis • topic • transmit • ultimate • unique • visible • voluntary

adapt
A family which has organized itself to run smoothly in the absence of one member must repeatedly adapt to incorporate the absent member when he or she returns home.

adult
In spite of this, however, differences in infant and adult mortality rates between social classes have widened.

advocate
I am surprised that many dentists don't advocate the use of fluoride tablets.

aid
Work is very rarely performed by a man without the aid of some machinery and correspondingly machines rarely function for very long without human intervention.

channel
The report notes the large investment in tourist facilities on the other side of the English Channel including the huge Euro Disney complex and its related transport infrastructure.

chemical
The chemical industry makes a crucial contribution to our health and prosperity and to the protection of the environment.

classic
From the moment you sit back in the Orion's roomy interior, you'll know how it feels to drive a classic car.

comprehensive
As with all insurance policies, you should check with your insurance agent to make sure what perils are included under the comprehensive coverage of your auto insurance policy.

comprise
Study bedrooms are single occupancy and comprise bed, desk, chair, wardrobe and shelving; all have Internet access.

confirm
I have not heard back from you since then, and I wondered if you could please confirm.

contrary
Contrary to popular opinion, there are those who like to leave school as soon as possible to start their working life.

convert
Economic uncertainty and a return to a monthly inflation rate of over 24 per cent had prompted an increasing trend for people to convert their assets into gold and dollars.

couple
His three customers on the plane were a woman who had changed her travel plans at the last minute and a married couple starting a world tour.

decade
Throughout that decade Vox were one of the few British guitar 'names', and certain models from that era have become much sought-after by collectors.

definite
One of the hardest problems to confront, though, is the correct use of "the" (the definite article), a word which has no direct equivalent in many languages.

deny
Nobody, however, would deny that there is a growing gap between those who rely for the majority of their income on state benefits and the average working population.

differentiate
While very young children can differentiate the past from the present, many have considerable difficulty in differentiating between two periods in the past.

dispose
That means we are looking at having to dispose of around two and a half million tons of wet sewage every year by the end of the century.

dynamic
Mrs Thatcher also believed that the publicly owned industries were inefficient and an obstacle to the creation of a more dynamic and adaptive economy.

eliminate
As for the future he said: 'We are constantly striving for ways in which to improve quality and efficiency and to eliminate waste and mediocrity.

empirical
The empirical probability of an event is an "estimate" that the event will happen based on how often the event occurs after collecting data or running an experiment.

equip
Course content has been selected to give graduates the necessary knowledge, skills and experience to equip them for careers in software development.

extract
One teacher showed a brief extract from a historical film that had proved a great box office success.

file
The file should not be edited but may be deleted or renamed as part of your database management.

finite
A 'renewable energy source' is one which does not depend on finite reserves of either fossil or nuclear fuels.

foundation
I'd finished my foundation year earlier that summer and, although I'd been offered a fulltime place, and grant, to do my Fine Art degree in painting, I decided not to continue.

globe
Modern technology pushes our wilderness completely off the inhabited globe into space.

grade
The studies went well and Grace got the top grade in her 'A' Level maths exam.

guarantee
The easily identifiable tartan mark is your guarantee that the salmon you are buying is genuinely Scottish and produced in accordance with a stringent set of quality standards.

hierarchy
Thus, a principal function of top management is to co-ordinate and monitor the efforts of those lower down the hierarchy.

identical
In many parts of the tropics there are mass spawnings of marine worms at the full moon at identical periods each year, the water glowing phosphorescent green during these times.

ideology
Given that ideology represents an individual's values and beliefs, it makes sense that those with different ideological views have more confidence in some institutions than others.

infer
If someone slams a door, you can infer that he or she is upset about something.

innovate
Economics also dictates change, especially the need for large businesses to innovate and to be entrepreneurs.

insert
You can insert comments into assembly language programs by preceding them with a semi-slash.

intervene
Nobody will believe that governments are likely to intervene when exchange rates move toward the edge of their bands.

isolate
Streptomycin is more stable than penicillin and so it was easier to isolate and manufacture.

media
It is commonplace that children now seem to grow up alarmingly fast, education and the media combining to erode the apparent gap between the generations.

mode
Step straight from a working day into the party mode.

paradigm
Much of modern sociology lacks a paradigm and consequently fails to qualify as science.

phenomenon
The problem of deposits on soft contact lenses is not a recent or unique phenomenon.

priority
Part of my later training had been at the hands of an ex-SAS instructor whose absolute priority for survival was evading the enemy.

prohibit
Some governments rewrote their constitutions to restrict, or prohibit altogether, private or foreign participation in their oil industries.

publication
While every effort is made to ensure the accuracy of printed information, readers should be aware that this is an internal newsletter and not an official publication.

quote
'To quote the famous American philosopher Yogi Berra (of baseball fame),' he said, 'It ain't over till it's over.'

release
The hour-long tape is available through golf pro shops before its nationwide retail release.

reverse
The Government's underlying aim is now to get growth back into the economy so as to reverse the rising trend in unemployment.

simulate
The intention has been to stimulate interest within the British Airways engineering community towards AI based solutions to engineering diagnostics problems.

sole
In total, 1 in 5 old people were dependent upon state benefit for their sole income.

somewhat
Although a private man and somewhat of a loner, he worked tirelessly for the department both in a teaching and administrative capacity.

submit
Every local authority was required to submit a county development plan for acceptance by the Welsh Office before funds were released.

successor
What is known of his life comes mainly from a memorial sermon preached by his friend and successor as bishop, George Rust, and from his own books.

survive
The competitive nature of capitalism means that only the largest and most wealthy companies will survive and prosper.

thesis
Her thesis was that cultural and physical diversity was important in the life of a city, and she charged planners with pursuing policies which had the effect of eradicating it.

topic
This general theme is even more relevant now to the field of special educational needs than it was three years ago when the initial decision about the conference topic was made.

transmit
The tendons are like cords that transmit the force of the muscle to other parts of the limb skeleton.

ultimate
A British international cap has long been regarded as the ultimate achievement for the amateur golfer.

unique
At Etihad we apply our unique vision of air travel – personalised, hospitable and very luxurious – to our loyalty programme.

visible
Please look into the matter and see what can be done to make the lights visible again.

voluntary
There is a danger that a voluntary organisation can take on more than it can handle and consequently overstretch its resources.

Gap Fill Exercises - Sublist 7

The exercises presented here give you an opportunity to review the words in Sublist 7.

Use the words from the box to complete the sentences below.

```
advocate - comprehensive - confirm - deny - file
grade - hierarchy - intervene - quote - release
```

1. Nobody will believe that governments are likely to _____when exchange rates move toward the edge of their bands.

2. The hour-long tape is available through golf pro shops before its nationwide retail _____.

3. As with all insurance policies, you should check with your insurance agent to make sure what perils are included under the _____coverage of your auto insurance policy.

4. Nobody, however, would _____that there is a growing gap between those who rely for the majority of their income on state benefits and the average working population.

5. 'To _____the famous American philosopher Yogi Berra (of baseball fame),' he said, 'It ain't over till it's over.'

6. Thus, a principal function of top management is to co-ordinate and monitor the efforts of those lower down the _____.

7. The studies went well and Grace got the top _____in her 'A' Level maths exam.

8. I have not heard back from you since then, and I wondered if you could please _____.

9. I am surprised that many dentists don't _____the use of fluoride tablets.

10. The _____should not be edited but may be deleted or renamed as part of your database management.

abandon • accompany • accumulate • ambiguous • append • appreciate • arbitrary • automate • bias chart • clarify • commodity • complement • conform • contemporary • contradict • crucial • currency denote • detect • deviate • displace • drama • eventual • exhibit • exploit • fluctuate • guideline • highlight implicit • induce • inevitable • infrastructure • inspect • intense • manipulate • minimize • nuclear • offset paragraph • plus • practitioner • predominant • prospect • radical • random • reinforce • restore • revise schedule • tense • terminate • theme • thereby • uniform • vehicle • via • virtual • visual • widespread

abandon
Trading in dammars, incense wood and rattans sometimes yields financial returns so high that the people abandon cultivation of edible crops in their favour.

accompany
Physical symptoms, such as headaches or bowel problems, usually accompany the mental symptoms in those who are sensitive to something in their diet or environment.

accumulate
It is a matter of common observation that shingle tends to accumulate on the higher parts of the beach while the lower parts are essentially sandy.

ambiguous
An ambiguous phrase is one that is not easy to understand, and often could be interpreted different ways.

append
One stratagem a fiction writer can employ to persuade his audience that he is writing fact is to append yards of references.

appreciate
One thing I did appreciate in almost all the French and German restaurants I ate in, was the happy absence of Muzak.

arbitrary
Because the arbitrary pension ages of 60 and 65 have been adopted as customary retirement ages, women have been forced to retire five years earlier than men.

automate
Six of Japan's 10 electric-power companies are cooperating with Hitachi and Toshiba (the country's biggest nuclear power-plant makers) to automate dangerous work.

bias
This is not a result of sampling bias on our part, as all known sites of geothermal silica deposits were sampled.

chart
Once the chart is complete you will be able to see your findings at a glance.

clarify
I hope that the government will clarify their stance and reassure the people of Scotland that we are not to be the nuclear dustbin of the world.

commodity
In the following year, having recently seen hemp grown and processed for use in the textile industry in Holland, he asked if this commodity was grown in the north of England.

complement
In certain worms, for example, there is loss of DNA from some cells, only the future germ cells retaining the full complement of DNA.

conform
These changes, and the need for Britain to conform with EC legislation, gave rise to ever more comprehensive labelling regulations.

contemporary
During my undergraduate studies, I had become particularly interested in the linguistic parts of the syllabus, and I opted for what was then called 'Syllabus B'— a set of courses which contained a large amount of language work, more historical than contemporary.

contradict
This does not contradict the general guideline that children be given the opportunity to make choices or to discuss reasons.

crucial
The economic structure of the market in assessing the competitive effect of a merger is crucial.

currency
If a country is prone to high inflation then its currency will have to be devalued at regular intervals to maintain the price competitiveness of its exports.

denote
The word 'estate' is often used to denote the whole of a man's proprietary rights, more especially after his death.

detect
The chlorine we detect in the rivers has actually come from the ocean.

deviate
While most middle-class women say they dislike housework and most working-class women say they like or don't mind it, there are some in each class group who deviate from this pattern.

displace
Other hopes have centred on ethanol taking the place of petroleum — but fuel crops must not displace food.

drama
In fact, this need to turn contemporary life into drama had been the defining characteristic of his work since "Portrait of a Lady".

eventual
She made it through to the final and an eventual 6th place overall showed just how much she had learned and improved that year.

exhibit
Politicians and diplomats frequently exhibit these characteristics when dealing with foreign affairs.

exploit
Developing countries will remain poor unless they can exploit natural resources to their own advantage.

fluctuate
We get some glimpse of what conditions would be like without water by observing modern deserts, which commonly fluctuate from +45°C to around zero, in the course of twelve hours!

guideline
As well as representing the values and standards of the BBC, the Editorial Guidelines reflect the relevant provisions of the Ofcom Broadcasting Code.

highlight
Walks are scheduled to take place all over the country taking routes which highlight various problems which have arisen from landowners denying access to the countryside.

implicit
Many of the changes in the National Health Service over recent years have had an implicit, if not explicit, goal of strengthening the notion of line management.

induce
Soft lighting is deliberately used for example by restaurateurs to induce a feeling of relaxation, enhance the enjoyment of the meal, and promote pleasurable conversation.

inevitable
British Rail fares are already the highest in Europe, but further increases of this scale will be inevitable without a change in government policy.

infrastructure
We support the location of new industrial and commercial developments in areas already well-served by good transport infrastructure and public transport.

inspect
He used to cycle from village to village visiting farms to inspect the animals and then on market days he would try to conclude deals between the farmers.

intense

Ending months of intense speculation, Prime Minister John Major announced on March 11 that the general election would be held on April 9.

manipulate

Four major banks agreed to plead guilty to trying to manipulate foreign exchange rates and six were fined nearly $US6 billion in yet another settlement in a global probe into the $US5-trillion-a-day market.

minimize

The amount of caffeine should be reduced gradually, over a period of two to three weeks, to minimize withdrawal reactions.

nuclear

The term nuclear family was developed in the western world to distinguish the family group consisting of parents and their children, from what is known as an extended family.

offset

A carbon offset is a credit for greenhouse gas reductions achieved by one party that can be purchased and used to compensate (offset) the emissions of another party.

paragraph

The unity and coherence of ideas among sentences is what constitutes a paragraph.

plus

Women's Running magazine was praised by readers after featuring a plus-size model jogging on its latest cover to prove that athletes come in all shapes and sizes.

practitioner

In the UK it is likely that your first point of contact for most medical services will be your Family Doctor or General Practitioner.

predominant

Farms devoted to arable crops are predominant in the eastern part of England.

prospect

There was no incentive to move, for the bus queues were twice as long as usual; the rush-hour had started, and the prospect of the long wait in the rain did not appeal.

radical

Over the years, scientists have envisioned a few radical ways to combat global warming including the placing of wave-powered pumps in the Pacific Ocean.

random

A random sequence of events, has no order and does not follow an intelligible pattern.

reinforce

Anti-abortionists have launched a vigorous campaign to reinforce the constitutional ban.

restore
Privacy and data protection can restore consumer confidence in the digital society.

revise
Community care reforms in the United Kingdom have been advanced as a genuine attempt to revise existing patterns of service and produce more effective care for those in need.

schedule
Most choreographers either have other responsibilities (as a company director, for instance) or are themselves tied to the strict daily schedule of a performer.

tense
Being tense and finding little or no time to relax is an important stress indicator.

terminate
Generally, an employer must not terminate an employee's employment unless they have given the employee written notice of termination, or payment in lieu of that notice.

theme
Theme restaurants are restaurants in which the concept of the restaurant takes priority over everything else, influencing the architecture, food, music, and even the overall 'feel'.

thereby
One way of trying to prevent a hang-over is to drink a couple of glasses of water after each alcoholic drink, thereby preventing dehydration.

uniform
A body is said to have uniform motion if it covers equal distances in equal intervals of time, no matter how small these time intervals may be.

vehicle
The two men received sentences of nine months for allowing themselves to be carried in a stolen vehicle.

via
The slower cross-country route from Peterborough to Harwich can take longer and involve more changes than going via London, but avoids changing trains and stations in London.

virtual
Virtual reality will turn the weekly supermarket shop into a pleasure to be enjoyed from the comfort of the armchair.

visual
Every bend reveals another staggering visual feast and it is all to do with the light, the dynamic mountain ridges, the pure white sandy beaches and the undisturbed peace.

widespread
Nevertheless, there was widespread criticism that the relief operation was badly organized.

Gap Fill Exercises - Sublist 8

The gap presented here give you an opportunity to review the words in Sublist 8.

Use the words from the box to complete the sentences below.

> ambiguous - automate - conform - fluctuate - guideline
> inevitable - paragraph - prospect - reinforce - via

1. An _____phrase is one that is not easy to understand, and often could be interpreted different ways.

2. The slower cross-country route from Peterborough to Harwich can take longer and involve more changes than going _____London, but avoids changing trains and stations in London.

3. Six of Japan's 10 electric-power companies are cooperating with Hitachi and Toshiba (the country's biggest nuclear power-plant makers) to _____dangerous work.

4. As well as representing the values and standards of the BBC, the Editorial _____reflect the relevant provisions of the Ofcom Broadcasting Code.

5. British Rail fares are already the highest in Europe, but further increases of this scale will be _____without a change in government policy.

6. We get some glimpse of what conditions would be like without water by observing modern deserts, which commonly _____ from +45°C to around zero, in the course of twelve hours!

7. There was no incentive to move, for the bus queues were twice as long as usual; the rush-hour had started, and the _____of the long wait in the rain did not appeal.

8. These changes, and the need for Britain to _____with EC legislation, gave rise to ever more comprehensive labelling regulations.

9. Anti-abortionists have launched a vigorous campaign to _____the constitutional ban.

10.
The unity and coherence of ideas among sentences is what constitutes a _____.

Sublist 9

accommodate • analogy • anticipate • assure • attain • behalf • bulk • cease • coherent • coincide commence • compatible • concurrent • confine • controversy • converse • device • devote • diminish distort • duration • erode • ethic • format • founded • inherent • insight • integral • intermediate • manual mature • mediate • medium • military • minimal • mutual • norm • overlap • passive • portion preliminary • protocol • qualitative • refine • relax • restrain • revolution • rigid • route • scenario • sphere subordinate • supplement • suspend • team • temporary • trigger • unify • violate • vision

accommodate
Directly below the library, the spacious facilities accommodate the ever-expanding student population with a cafeteria, large function room, lounge bar and committee rooms.

analogy
People have an innate tendency to understand the true meaning when one concept has been compared to another and so using an analogy can be very useful when explaining things.

anticipate
Since we anticipate strong demand for this new product range we recommend you to place your first order as soon as possible.

assure
I want to assure you that the safety of our students, staff, and our parents is foremost in our minds when we make decisions about the opening and closing times of our school.

attain
The patient must understand the achievable range of blood glucose and have the knowledge and confidence to attain that range consistently by balancing the dose of insulin with diet, exercise and inter-current illness.

behalf
On behalf of my family I would like to thank you for a memorable birthday party celebration in your hotel.

bulk
Boeing has warned airlines that flying bulk shipments of lithium-ion batteries can cause fires capable of destroying airplanes.

cease
A popular theory is that the body's genetic material 'wears out', accumulating more and more errors until the body's cells cease to function altogether.

coherent
This will lead to the breakdown of a coherent local system of education which seeks to meet the needs of the whole learning community.

coincide
The solar eclipse this year will coincide with two other events – the super moon, when the full or new moon is at its closest point to Earth, and the spring equinox.

commence
I wish my membership at your gymnasium to commence from the first of August.

compatible
In their quest for greater public acceptability, science museums have tended to move in two different, and not always compatible, directions.

concurrent
This year there are not two, but three concurrent contemporary art fairs around the city.

confine
Trade unions should confine themselves to the business of wages and conditions.

controversy
Elsewhere, particularly in the remoter upland areas, the issue which has aroused most controversy has been the purchase of second homes as weekend or holiday retreats.

converse
The converse of "If it is raining then the grass is wet" is "If the grass is wet then it is raining.

device
Medical device companies operate in a complex global regulatory environment with continually changing standards.

devote
As the total area allocated to these crops increased, so the amount of time and land which a family could devote to food crop production for its own consumption often diminished.

diminish
When you repress or bottle up so much anger, you simultaneously diminish other feelings, including love and affection.

distort
In fact the maximum output of the amplifier is just over 100mW and the headphones will begin to distort long before the amplifier does with high level inputs.

duration
I advised her to take four to six garlic capsules a day for the duration of the treatment which we hoped would not be too prolonged.

erode
Sudden movements in exchange and interest rates can erode profit margins, strain your cash flow and shrink overall profits.

ethic
Japan's fierce work ethic has led to the term – karoshi – which means death from overwork and has resulted in cases where office workers put in up to 114 hours of overtime a month.

format
When we format cells in Excel, we change the appearance of a number without changing the number itself.

founded
All of the companies listed on www.foundedinbangladesh.com were founded in Bangladesh in the 21st century.

inherent
A skier has the duty to ski at all times in a manner that avoids injury to the skier and others and to be aware of the inherent dangers and risks of skiing.

insight
Their approach now is to try and find out where and when the protein is made during limb development, in the hope that this will provide some insight as to how the gene works.

integral
Contact tracing has become an integral part of the control of infectious disease.

intermediate
The conversion of various food group products into a two-carbon molecule of acetyl coenzyme is called the 'intermediate step' because it links other pathways to Krebs' Cycle.

manual
A sustained campaign for pensions for manual workers began in the late 19th century.

mature
Vigorous rootstocks produce large trees that will give high yields even on poorer soils, provide shade and wildlife habitats, and are magnificent specimens when mature.

mediate
If your two best friends aren't speaking to each other, you might find yourself trying to mediate a peace accord between them.

medium
The press always has been a medium of propaganda as well as a medium of information.

military
Merchants trading overseas had to cover the diplomatic and even military expenses which in later centuries would be met by their governments.

minimal
In the less well-developed countries, where warnings of impending storms are poor and precautions minimal, entire villages can be swept away and vast communities decimated.

mutual
In fact, I knew the principals of all these nurseries personally, and enjoyed a mutual respect with them.

norm
Two cars per family is the norm in most suburban communities.

overlap
Genetic overlap between Alzheimer's disease (AD) and two significant cardiovascular disease risk factors has been identified by researchers.

passive
They may also feel that they have no right to put their children at risk by making them passive smokers.

portion
Portion control is an important concept when you're trying to lose weight and keep it off.

preliminary
A Preliminary Criminal History Evaluation is a non-mandatory, non-binding evaluation of an individual's self-reported criminal history.

protocol
The Kyoto Protocol is an international agreement which commits its parties by setting internationally binding emission reduction targets.

qualitative
To succeed in an increasingly competitive world economy, they have to make a qualitative leap in ability to use modern technologies, production processes and telecommunications.

refine
Hypotheses, then, help us to refine theory by bringing more details into consideration in areas of research which may previously have only been explored in a rather sketchy way.

relax
Imagine a haven far away from the hustle and bustle of the city…a private world where you can pamper yourself in unparalleled luxury…and relax in surroundings of timeless beauty.

restrain
Certain public schools were found to be far too quick to restrain or isolate unruly children against their will, leaving hundreds with injuries.

revolution
The Industrial Revolution was a period during which predominantly agrarian, rural societies in Europe and America became industrial and urban.

rigid
He grew even more rigid and uncompromising as he got older.

route
Before it was called Route 66 this corridor was traversed by the National Old Trails
Highway, one of the country's first transcontinental highways.

scenario
Participants also suggested including territorial planning to guarantee the most fertile lands
for agriculture, since several scenarios showed drastic urban expansion.

sphere
In attempting to understand the role of the media in society, it is useful to use the concept
of the 'public sphere' as an ideal, serving as a model or guide for what the media could be.

subordinate
Even if you are hoping to work in a subordinate position for the very person who is
interviewing you, you do not need to take a passive role in the interview.

supplement
The need to supplement the family income motivates some parents to encourage children
to go out and earn a wage as soon as possible.

suspend
Management might suspend all negotiations about pay and conditions until employees
agree to work normally during the bargaining.

team
England boss Graham Taylor has admitted for the first time that his team flopped in the
European Championship finals because they weren't fit enough.

temporary
I assured myself that it would be only temporary and I would soon be in a flat again, but
'temporary' turned out to be five years.

trigger
The weather can trigger headaches or migraine for some people.

unify
Microsoft supremo Bill Gates is doing more to unify Unix than any other single human
being in the last five years.

violate
Submissive behaviour is defined as coming from a belief that your rights and needs are less
important than other people's and that others can violate them.

vision
Intellectual risk takers are the life blood of our school system and provide the vision which
we so much need.

Gap Fill Exercises - Sublist 9

The exercises presented here give you an opportunity to review the words in Sublist 9.

Use the words from the box to complete the sentences below.

```
analogy - behalf - compatible - device - mature
portion - protocol - restrain - route - vision
```

1. Medical _____companies operate in a complex global regulatory environment with continually changing standards.

2. Vigorous rootstocks produce large trees that will give high yields even on poorer soils, provide shade and wildlife habitats, and are magnificent specimens when _____.

3. The Kyoto _____is an international agreement which commits its parties by setting internationally binding emission reduction targets.

4. _____control is an important concept when you're trying to lose weight and keep it off.

5. People have an innate tendency to understand the true meaning when one concept has been compared to another and so using an _____can be very useful when explaining things.

6. On _____of my family I would like to thank you for a memorable birthday party celebration in your hotel.

7. In their quest for greater public acceptability, science museums have tended to move in two different, and not always _____, directions.

8. Before it was called _____66 this corridor was traversed by the National Old Trails Highway, one of the country's first transcontinental highways.

9. Intellectual risk takers are the life blood of our school system and provide the _____ which we so much need.

10.
Certain public schools were found to be far too quick to _____or isolate unruly children against their will, leaving hundreds with injuries.

Sublist 10

adjacent • albeit • assemble • collapse • colleague • compile • conceive • convince • depress • encounter enormous • forthcoming • incline • integrity • intrinsic • invoke • levy • likewise • nonetheless notwithstanding • odd • ongoing • panel • persist • pose • reluctance • so-called • straightforward undergo • whereby

adjacent
If you like the idea of calling the Queen your neighbour then a luxury apartment block adjacent to Buckingham Palace will come onto the market early next year.

albeit
The recipe called for a tablespoon of saffron, which made it very tasty, albeit rather expensive.

assemble
It's often joked that Ikea's labyrinthine stores and hard-to-assemble furniture can ruin relationships because of the stress caused by the whole process of shopping and assembling.

collapse
A bridge collapse in Southern California forced the closure of Interstate 10 which is a main roadway between Southern California and Phoenix.

colleague
Colleagues are those explicitly united in a common purpose and respecting each other's abilities to work toward that purpose.

compile
Many attempts have been made to compile a genealogical tree showing the relationships of these animals to one another and to man.

conceive
It is certainly possible to conceive of many solutions to this problem but the most viable ones involve the help of not only the government but society as a whole.

convince
It is sometimes very difficult to convince people of the obvious.

depress
Future sales of our common stock could depress our market price and diminish the value of your investment.

encounter
Doctors encounter people who take up an undue amount of their time with trivial matters.

enormous
Policies and tax preferences continue to favour the affluent and, most strikingly, it has resulted in an enormous wealth gap between white households and households of African-Americans.

forthcoming
For the purposes of this forthcoming report, we define population health management as: The proactive management of the health of a given population by a defined network of providers who are financially linked, in partnership with community stakeholders (e.g. social workers, visiting nurses, caregivers and so on.).

incline
Sit-ups, crunches, leg raises and knee tucks are all possible on this simple piece of equipment, and as the stomach muscles become stronger the angle of incline is increased so as to bring gravity into play.

integrity
A person with integrity has the ability to pull everything together, to make it all happen no matter how challenging the circumstances.

intrinsic
In general, the intrinsic elements of literary works include the theme, plot, characterizations, setting, tension, the atmosphere, the central narrative, and style.

invoke
Palaeontologists have typically tried to find particular reasons for major changes in the history of life, and in particular to invoke the idea of evolution by natural selection; the idea, crudely stated, that 'inferior' creatures are replaced by their superiors.

levy
In America, tax debts that go unpaid may lead the Inland Revenue Service (IRS) to take possession of a taxpayer's property in a procedure called an IRS levy.

likewise
Since he had studied hard and graduated from university, he hoped that his rather lazy brother could perform likewise.

nonetheless
Although they discovered they had hardly a single taste in common, he was nonetheless a witty and amusing host and she found herself laughing in a way she had not done for a considerable time.

notwithstanding
This provision shall apply notwithstanding anything contained to the contrary contained in this act or any other law.

odd
A British lawmaker is defending claiming 9 pence ($0.14) on expenses for a short car journey, saying such claims may look "odd" but the mileage adds up.

ongoing
The ongoing debate over e-cigarettes and whether or not they are as harmful has continued to generate interest.

panel
The panel interview is often the final interview full of judges judging your body language, every last accomplishment and even what questions you ask.

persist
This feature allows the virus to persist in the environment even though its host, the insect larva, may be present for only a few weeks during the year.

pose
The reluctance of people to give up their car in favour of public transport may well pose the biggest problem to solving the issues of traffic congestion.

reluctance
The fact that many farms were the 'family home', often going back three or four generations, was another reason for the reluctance to sell.

so-called
Supermarkets' so-called healthy ranges of food contain the equivalent of up to 22.5 teaspoons of sugar, a recent investigation has revealed.

straightforward
The children make sure I never have a straightforward day.

undergo
Rather than increasing the sentence, three appeal court judges substituted a three-year probation order requiring him to undergo treatment or counselling.

whereby
Surrogacy is the practice whereby a woman (the surrogate mother) carries a child for another person as the result of an agreement prior to conception that the child should be handed over to her after the birth.

Gap Fill Exercises - Sublist 10

The exercises presented here give you an opportunity to review the words in Sublist 10.

Use the words from the box to complete the sentences below.

> adjacent - assemble - collapse - compile - convince
> depress - notwithstanding - odd - so-called - whereby

1. Many attempts have been made to _____a genealogical tree showing the relationships of these animals to one another and to man.

2. Supermarkets' _____healthy ranges of food contain the equivalent of up to 22.5 teaspoons of sugar, a recent investigation has revealed.

3. Surrogacy is the practice _____a woman (the surrogate mother) carries a child for another person as the result of an agreement prior to conception that the child should be handed over to her after the birth.

4. Future sales of our common stock could _____our market price and diminish the value of your investment.

5. It is sometimes very difficult to _____people of the obvious.

6. This provision shall apply _____anything contained to the contrary contained in this act or any other law.

7. If you like the idea of calling the Queen your neighbour then a luxury apartment block _____ to Buckingham Palace will come onto the market early next year.

8. A bridge _____in Southern California forced the closure of Interstate 10 which is a main roadway between Southern California and Phoenix.

9. It's often joked that Ikea's labyrinthine stores and hard-to-_____furniture can ruin relationships because of the stress caused by the whole process of shopping and assembling.

10. A British lawmaker is defending claiming 9 pence ($0.14) on expenses for a short car journey, saying such claims may look "_____" but the mileage adds up.

FINAL REVIEW

Test 1

For the first time, conscious memories have been implanted into the minds of mice while they sleep. The same 1. _____ could one day be used to 2. _____ memories in people who have 3. _____ traumatic events.

When we sleep, our brain replays the day's activities. The pattern of brain activity 4. _____ by mice when they explore a new 5. _____ during the day, for example, will reappear, speeded up, while the animal sleeps. This is thought to be the brain practising an activity – an essential part of learning. People who miss out on sleep do not learn as well as those who get a good night's rest, and when the replay 6. _____ is disrupted in mice, so too is their ability to remember what they learned the 7. _____ day.

Karim Benchenane and his 8. _____ at the Industrial Physics and Chemistry Higher Educational 9. _____ in Paris, France, hijacked this 10. _____ to 11. _____ new memories in sleeping mice (Nature Neuroscience). The 12. _____ 13. _____ the rodents' place cells – neurons that fire in 14. _____ to being in or thinking about a 15. _____ place. These cells are thought to help us form 16. _____ maps; last year their discoverers won a Nobel Prize..

> alter - area - colleagues - create - exhibited - institution - internal - previous - process (2x)
> response - specific - targeted - team - technique - undergone

Test 2

A new 1. _____ to quantum mechanics 2. _____ some of its most famous oddities, including the 3. _____ of quantum objects being both a wave and a particle, and existing in multiple states at once.

In short, the 4. _____ 5. _____ the wave 6. _____ and demotes the 7. _____ that describes it. In its place are a huge but 8. _____ number of ordinary, 9. _____ worlds, whose jostling explains the weird effects 10. _____ ascribed to quantum mechanics.

Quantum 11. _____ was dreamed up to describe the strange behaviour of particles like atoms and electrons. For nearly a century, physicists have explained the peculiarities of their quantum properties – such as wave-particle duality and indeterminism – by 12. _____ an 13. _____ called the wave 14. _____, which exists in a superposition of all possible states at once right up until someone observes it, at which point it is said to "15. _____" into a single state.

Physicist Erwin Schrödinger famously 16. _____ this idea by imagining a cat in a box that is both dead and alive until someone opens the box to check on it. The probability that the cat will 17. _____ is given by the Schrödinger 18. _____, which describes all the possible states that the wave 19. _____ can take.

> approach (2x) - collapse - concept - eliminates - entity - equation (2x) - finite - function (3x)
> illustrated - invoking - normally - parallel - removes - survive - theory

FINAL REVIEW

Task 3

Talking to yourself used to be a strictly private pastime. That's no longer the case – 1. _____have eavesdropped on our 2. _____monologue for the first time. The 3. _____is a step towards helping people who cannot 4. _____speak 5. _____with the outside world.

"If you're reading 6. _____in a newspaper or a book, you hear a voice in your own head," says Brian Pasley at the University of California, Berkeley. "We're trying to decode the brain activity related to that voice to 7. _____a 8. _____ prosthesis that can allow someone who is paralysed or locked in to speak."

When you hear someone speak, sound waves activate sensory neurons in your inner ear. These neurons pass information to 9. _____of the brain where different 10. _____of the sound are 11. _____and 12. _____as words.

In a 13. _____study, Pasley and his 14. _____recorded brain activity in people who already had electrodes implanted in their brain to treat epilepsy, while they listened to speech. The 15. _____found that certain neurons in the brain's temporal lobe were only active in 16. _____to certain 17. _____of sound, such as a 18. _____frequency.

achievement - areas - aspects (2x) - colleagues - communicate - create - extracted - internal
interpreted - medical - physically - previous - researchers - response - specific - team - text

Task 4

They 1. _____that what was a 1-in-100-year event without 2. _____warming had become a 1-in-80-year event. In other words, human emissions made the extreme levels of rainfall experienced in south-east England 25 per cent more likely.

The 3. _____'s results were 4. _____online on 30 April, just two months after the flooding abated. To speed things up even more, a 5. _____called European Climate and Weather Events: 6. _____and 7. _____(EUCLEIA), led by Stott and 8. _____by the European Union, will test a new system. Instead of waiting for an event to happen, the idea is to 9. _____seasonal forecasts, which are done a month or more ahead of time, into the climate models.

"One of the 10. _____EUCLEIA is looking at is to use forecast sea-surface temperatures," says Allen. Sea-surface temperature is an important driver of the weather, and because the oceans change temperature very slowly compared with the air and land, they form a key, 11. _____12. _____of seasonal forecasts.

In the new set-up, a real-world seasonal forecast driven by 13. _____on current sea-surface temperatures will be run alongside a 14. _____"no 15. _____warming" seasonal forecast, in which greenhouse gas emissions have been stripped out.

attribution - component - concluded - data - designs - funded - global (2x) - incorporate
interpretation - predictable - project - published - simulated - team

FINAL REVIEW

Entrepreneurial Impact: The Role of MIT - an extract from - is based on one of the largest surveys of entrepreneurial alumni from the Massachusetts Institute of Technology (MIT) ever conducted and presents the economic impact of companies founded by MIT alumni.

Task 5

Part A

1. _____ - and 2. _____ - 3. _____universities, especially 4. _____their entrepreneurial spinoffs, have a 5. _____6. _____on the 7. _____ of the United States and its fifty states. A new report on just one such university, the Massachusetts 8. _____of 9. ___, 10. _____conservatively that, if the active companies 11. _____by MIT graduates formed an independent nation, their 12. _____would make that nation at least the seventeenth-largest 13. _____in the world. A less-conservative direct extrapolation of the 14. _____15. _____16. _____boosts the numbers to 25,800 currently active companies 17. _____by MIT alumni that employ about 3.3 million people and 18. _____19. _____ world sales of $2 trillion, producing the 20. _____of the eleventh-largest 21. _____in the world.

> annual - data - dramatic - economies - economy (2x) - equivalent - founded (2x) - generate
> impact - indicates - institute - intensive - research - revenues - survey - technology (2x)
> underlying - via

Part B

These findings result from an 1. _____of MIT alumni-2. _____companies and the entrepreneurial 3. _____that fosters this new-company 4. _____. 5. _____by Edward B. Roberts and Charles Eesley of the MIT Sloan School of Management, the report is based on a 2003 6. _____of all living MIT alumni, with additional detailed 7. _____, including verification and updating of 8. _____and employment figures to 2006 from records of Compustat (public companies) and Dun & Bradstreet (private companies).

> analyzes - analysis - conducted - creation - environment - founded - revenue - survey

Part C

The 1. _____value of this study is to help us understand the entrepreneurial 2. _____that universities can have. We know that universities play an important 3. _____in many 4. _____, 5. _____6. _____ 7. _____through their 8. _____education, 9. _____and development, and many other spillovers, but universities also can 10. _____a 11. _____and programs that make entrepreneurship common. While MIT's leadership in developing successful entrepreneurs has been 12. _____anecdotally, this study - one of the largest 13. _____of entrepreneur alumni ever 14. ___- quantifies the 15. _____of MIT's entrepreneurship success. And, while MIT is more 16. _____in the programs it offers and in its historical 17. _____of entrepreneurship, it also provides a benchmark by which other 18. _____can gauge the 19. _____ 20. _____of their alumni entrepreneurs. The report also provides numerous examples of programs and practices that might be adopted, intact or 21. _____as needed, by other universities that 22. _____23. _entrepreneurial development

> conducted - core - create - creating - culture (2x) - economic (2x) - economies - enhanced
> evident - impact (4x) - institutions - modified - research - role - seek - surveys - ultimate
> unique

FINAL REVIEW

Being Fluent with Information Technology (1999) – The National Academies Press

Task 6

Part A

In today's workplace, information 1. _____ is increasingly common. If the nation is to 2. _____ the
3. _____ 4. _____ from its 5. _____ in information 6. _____ a 7. _____ pool 8. _____ of using it
9. _____ is necessary. It is 10. _____ that 11. _____ who work with information and knowledge (so-
called "knowledge workers") need to understand the ubiquitous office information technologies, but it
is also true that few 12. _____ classifications 13. _____ no knowledge of information 14. _____ at all.
For example, the clerk in a retail 15. _____ at one time had only to know how to use a cash 16. _____.
Today, the same clerk can come into 17. _____ with inventory systems, order tracking, and 18. _ card
and other business systems, which are becoming more sophisticated and 19. _____. In the
manufacturing industry, many 20. _____ "blue-collar" workers must cope with a variety of
manufacturing systems for tracking materials, parts inventory and production, 21. _____ control, and
online 22. _____ and 23. _____.

> appropriately - benefit - capable - contact - credit - establishment - individuals - integrated
> investments - job - labour - manuals - maximum - obtain - obvious - procedures - process
> register - require - technology (3x) - traditionally

Part B

Though a company must train its employees in the use of its business systems, it is naïve to consider
such training as a one-time activity. The systems are upgraded frequently and become more 1. _____.
Opportunities to apply information 2. _____ to business problems and opportunities to 3. _____
existing information 4. _____ solutions continue, 5. _ a continual training mission. 6. _____, this
training 7. _____ is greatly simplified if the 8. _____ pool is already well educated in information
9. _____, since employees come up to speed faster and 10. _____ less training 11. _____. Further, they
will probably 12. _____ existing systems more fully and 13. _____ to upgrades better. Employee
productivity is directly 14. _____ by the employees' knowledge of information 15. _____.

> adapt - affected - complex - implying - integrate - labour - obviously - overall - require - task
> technology (4x) - utilize

ANSWERS

Page 3
1. team 2. networked 3. computer 4. tasks 5. similarly 6. communicate 7. abstract 8. institute 9. involved 10. cooperate. 11. published 12. devices 13. enabled 14. converting 15. computer 16. interpret 17. medical 18. colleagues 19. incorporating 20. team 21. computer 22. image 23. areas 24. involved

Page 4
1. energy 2. medical 3. decades 4. researchers 5. investigating 6. injuries 7. alter 8. physical 9. chemical 10. reactions 11. energy 12. revelation 13. compound 14. energy 15. affected 16. energy

Page 5
1. released 2. internal 3. documents 4. team 5. intelligence 6. security 7. experts 8. files 9. publishing 10. documents 11. team 12. range 13. regimes 14. principal 15. civil 16. team 17. team 18. documented 19. documents 20. researchers 21. team 22. purchasing

Page 6
1. analysing 2. encounters 3. duration 4. colleagues 5. data 6. revealed 7. dynamics 8. team 9. accurately 10. randomly 11. emergent 12. regulated 13. environment 14. equivalent 15. random 16. researchers 17. team

Page 12 - Sublist 1 1. assume 2. income 3. finance 4. benefit 5. identify 6. contract 7. area 8. environment 9. concept 10. evident

Page 18 - Sublist 2 1. survey 2. positive 3. chapter 4. potential 5. affect 6. purchase 7. tradition 8. administrate 9. equate 10. assist

Page 24 - Sublist 3 1. partner 2. maximize 3. technique 4. circumstance 5. compensate 6. link 7. layer 8. alternative 9. consent 10. fund

Page 30 - Sublist 4 1. project 2. investigate 3. parallel 4. adequate 5. debate 6. regime 7. error 8. option 9. obvious 10. emerge

Page 36 - Sublist 5 1. consult 2. reject 3. fundamental 4. sustain 5. pursue 6. transit 7. expose 8. whereas 9. generation 10. margin

Page 42 - Sublist 6 1. incorporate 2. precede 3. attach 4. diverse 5. cooperate 6. reveal 7. incentive 8. exceed 9. federal 10. enhance

Page 48 - Sublist 7 1. intervene 2. release 3. comprehensive 4. deny 5. quote 6. hierarchy 7. grade 8. confirm 9. advocate 10. file

Page 54 - Sublist 8 1. ambiguous 2. via 3. automate 4. guideline 5. inevitable 6. fluctuate 7. prospect 8. conform 9. reinforce 10. paragraph

Page 60 - Sublist 9 1. device 2. mature 3. protocol 4. portion 5. analogy 6. behalf 7. compatible 8. route 9. vision 10. restrain

Page 64 - Sublist 10 1. compile 2. so-called 3. whereby 4. depress 5. convince 6. notwithstanding 7. adjacent 8. collapse 9. assemble 10. odd

ANSWERS - Final Review

Pages 65 - 68

Task 1
1. technique 2. alter 3. undergone 4. exhibited 5. area 6. process 7. previous 8. colleagues 9. institution 10. process 11. create 12. team 13. targeted 14. response 15. specific 16. internal

Task 2
1. approach 2. eliminates 3. concept 4. approach 5. removes 6. function 7. equation 8. finite 9. parallel 10. normally 11. theory 12. invoking 13. entity 14. function 15. collapse 16. illustrated 17. survive 18. equation 19. function

Task 3
1. researchers 2. internal 3. achievement 4. physically 5. communicate 6. text 7. create 8. medical 9. areas 10. aspects 11. extracted 12. interpreted 13. previous 14. colleagues 15. team 16. response 17. aspects 18. specific

Task 4
1. concluded 2. global 3. team 4. published 5. project 6. interpretation 7. attribution 8. funded 9. incorporate 10. designs 11. predictable 12. component 13. data 14. simulated 15. global

Task 5
Part A
1. research 2. technology 3. intensive 4. via 5. dramatic 6. impact 7. economies 8. institute 9. technology 10. indicates 11. founded 12. revenues 13. economy 14. underlying 15. survey 16. data 17. founded 18. generate 19. annual 20. equivalent 21. economy

Part B
1. analysis 2. founded 3. environment 4. creation 5. conducted 6. survey 7. analyzes 8. revenue

Part C
1. ultimate 2. impact 3. role 4. economies 5. creating 6. economic 7. impact 8. core 9. research 10. create 11. culture 12. evident 13. surveys 14. conducted 15. impact 16. unique 17. culture 18. institutions 19. economic 20. impact 21. modified 22. seek 23. enhanced

Task 6
Part A
1. technology 2. obtain 3. maximum 4. benefit 5. investments 6. technology 7. labour 8. capable 9. appropriately 10. obvious 11. individuals 12. job 13. require 14. technology 15. establishment 16. register 17. contact 18. credit 19. integrated 20. traditionally 21. process 22. manuals 23. procedures

Part B
1. complex 2. technology 3. integrate 4. technology 5. implying 6. obviously 7. task 8. labour 9. technology 10. require 11. overall 12. utilize 13. adapt 14. affected 15. technology

1st 1,000 words

A	along	away	bird	can	colour
a	already	**B**	bit	capital	come
able	also	back	black	car	command
about	although	bad	blood	care	common
above	always	ball	blow	carry	company
accept	among	bank	blue	case	compare
accord	amount	bar	board	catch	complete
account	ancient	base	boat	cause	concern
across	and	battle	body	centre	condition
act	animal	be	book	certain	connect
actual	another	bear	born	chance	consider
add	answer	beauty	both	change	contain
address	any	because	box	character	content
admit	appear	become	boy	charge	continue
adopt	apply	bed	branch	chief	control
advance	appoint	before	bread	child	corner
advantage	arise	begin	breadth	choose	cost
affair	arm	behind	break	church	could
afford	army	being	bridge	circle	council
after	around	believe	bright	city	count
again	arrive	belong	bring	claim	country
against	art	below	brother	class	course
age	article	beneath	build	clean	court
ago	as	beside	burn	clear	cover
agree	ask	best	business	clock	creature
air	association	better	but	close	cross
all	at	between	buy	club	crowd
allow	attack	beyond	by	coast	cry
almost	attempt	big	**C**	cold	current
alone	average	bill	call	college	custom

71

1st 1,000 words

cut

D

dance
danger
dare
dark
date
daughter
day
dead
deal
decide
declare
deep
degree
deliver
demand
describe
desert
desire
destroy
detail
determine
develop
die
difference
difficult
direct
discover
disease

distance
distinguish
district
divide
do
doctor
dog
door
double
doubt
down
draw
dream
dress
drive
drop
dry
due
during

E

each
ear
early
earth
east
easy
eat
edge
effect
effort

either
else
employ
end
enemy
English
enjoy
enough
enter
entire
equal
escape
even
evening
event
ever
every
everywhere
evil
example
excellent
except
exchange
exercise
exist
expect
expense
experience
experiment
explain

express
extend
eye

F

face
fact
factory
fail
fair
faith
fall
familiar
family
famous
farm
fashion
fast
father
favourite
favour
fear
feed
feel
fellow
few
field
figure
fill
find
fine

finger
finish
fire
first
fish
fit
fix
floor
flower
follow
food
for
force
foreign
forget
form
former
forth
fortune
forward
free
friend
from
front
full
further
future

G

gain
game

garden
gate
gather
general
gentle
get
give
glad
glass
go
God
gold
good
great
green
ground
group
grow
guard

H

habit
half
hall
hand
handle
hang
happen
happy
hard
hardly

1st 1,000 words

have	I	lady	local	mother	number
he	idea	land	long	motor	narrow
head	if	language	look	mountain	nation
health	impossible	large	lose	mouth	native
hear	in	last	lost	move	nature
heat	inch	late	lot	much	near
heaven	include	law	love	music	necessary
heavy	increase	lay	low	must	neck
help	indeed	lead	**M**	my	need
her	independent	learn	machine	mention	neighbour
here	influence	least	main	mere	neither
hide	instead	leave	make	metal	never
high	intend	left	man	middle	new
hill	interest	length	manner	might	next
his	into	less	manners	mile	night
history	introduce	let	many	mind	no
hold	iron	letter	march	mine	none
home	it	level	mark	minister	nor
honour	its	library	market	minute	north
hope	**J**	lie	marry	miss	not
horse	join	life	mass	modern	note
hot	judge	lift	material	moment	nothing
hour	just	light	matter	money	notice
house	**K**	like	may	month	now
how	keep	likely	me	more	nowhere
hullo	kill	limit	mean	moreover	**O**
human	kind	line	measure	morning	object
hurrah	know	listen	meet	most	observe
husband	**L**	little	member	**N**	occasion
I	lack	live	memory	name	of

1st 1,000 words

off	paint	pound	put	remember	say
offer	paper	poverty	**Q**	repeat	scale
office	part	power	quality	reply	scarce
often	party	practical	quarter	report	scene
oil	pass	prepare	quiet	represent	school
old	past	present	quite	respect	science
once	pay	preserve	**R**	rest	sea
one	peace	press	race	result	season
only	people	pretty	raise	return	seat
open	perfect	prevent	rank	rich	second
operation	perhaps	price	rate	ride	secret
opinion	permanent	print	rather	right	secretary
opportunity	permit	private	reach	ring	see
or	person	problem	read	rise	seem
order	picture	produce	ready	river	seize
ordinary	piece	product	real	road	sell
organize	place	production	reason	roll	send
other	plan	program	receive	room	sense
otherwise	plant	programme	recent	rough	separate
ought	play	progress	recognize	round	serious
ounce	please	promise	record	rule	serve
our	point	proof	red	ruler	set
out of	political	proper	reduce	run	settle
out	poor	propose	refuse	rush	several
over	popular	protect	regard	**S**	shadow
owe	population	prove	regular	safe	shake
own	position	provide	relation	sail	shall
P	possess	public	religion	same	shape
page	possible	pull	remain	save	share
pain	post	purpose	remark	saw	shave

1st 1,000 words

she	society	stick	sure	though	university
shine	soft	still	surface	thought	unless
shoe	soil	stock	surprise	through	until
shoot	some	stone	surround	throw	up
shore	son	stop	sweet	thus	upon
short	soon	store	system	time	use
should	sort	storm	**T**	to	usual
shoulder	sound	story	thing	today	**V**
show	south	straight	think	together	valley
side	space	strange	this	too	value
sight	speak	stream	table	top	various
sign	special	street	take	total	very
silence	speed	strength	talk	touch	view
silver	spend	stretch	taste	toward/s	village
simple	spirit	strike	teach	town	visit
since	spite	strong	tear	trade	voice
single	spot	struggle	tell	train	vote
sir	spread	study	term	travel	**W**
sister	spring	subject	terrible	tree	wait
sit	square	substance	test	trouble	walk
situation	stage	succeed	than	trust	wall
size	stand	such	that	truth	want
skill	standard	sudden	the	try	war
sky	start	suffer	their	turn	warn
sleep	state	suggest	them	type	waste
slight	station	summer	then	**U**	watch
slow	stay	sun	there	under	water
small	steal	supply	therefore	understand	wave
smile	steel	support	these	union	way
so	step	suppose	they	unite	we

75

1st 1,000 words

weak	whether	wild	with	worse	yesterday
wear	which	will	within	worth	yet
week	while	win	without	would	you
welcome	white	wind	woman	write	young
well	who	window	wonder	wrong	
west	whose	wing	wood	**Y**	
what	why	winter	word	year	
when	wide	wise	work	yellow	
where	wife	wish	world	yes	

2nd 1,000 words

A	apart	bake	bless	bus	charm
abroad	apologize	balance	blind	bush	cheap
absence	applaud	band	block	busy	cheat
absolutely	apple	barber	boast	butter	check
accident	approve	bare	boil	button	cheer
accuse	arch	bargain	bold	C	cheese
accustom	argue	barrel	bone	cage	chest
ache	arrange	basin	border	cake	chicken
admire	arrest	basket	borrow	calculate	chimney
adventure	arrow	bath	bottle	calm	Christmas
advertise	artificial	bay	bottom	camera	civilize
advice	ash	beak	bound	camp	clay
afraid	ashamed	beam	boundary	canal	clerk
afternoon	aside	bean	bow	cap	clever
agent	asleep	beard	bowl	cape	cliff
agriculture	astonish	beast	brain	captain	climb
ahead	attend	beat	brave	card	cloth
aim	attract	beg	brass	carriage	cloud
airplane	audience	behave	breakfast	cart	coal
alike	aunt	bell	breath	castle	coarse
alive	autumn	belt	bribe	cat	coat
aloud	avenue	bend	brick	cattle	coffee
altogether	avoid	berry	broad	caution	coin
ambition	awake	bicycle	brown	cave	collar
amongst	awkward	bind	brush	cent	collect
amuse	axe	birth	bucket	century	colony
anger	B	bite	bunch	ceremony	comb
angle	baby	bitter	bundle	chain	combine
annoy	bag	blade	burst	chair	comfort
anxiety	baggage	blame	bury	chalk	commerce

2nd 1,000 words

committee	crash	defeat	dozen	envy	film
companion	cream	defend	drag	essence	firm
compete	creep	delay	drawer	exact	flag
complain	crime	delicate	drink	examination	flame
complicated	critic	delight	drown	excess	flash
compose	crop	department	drum	excite	flat
confess	crown	depend	duck	excuse	flavor
confidence	cruel	descend	dull	explode	flesh
confuse	crush	deserve	dust	explore	float
congratulate	cultivate	desk	duty	extra	flood
conquer	cup	despair	**E**	extraordinary	flour
conscience	cupboard	devil	eager	extreme	flow
conscious	cure	diamond	earn	**F**	fly
convenience	curious	dictionary	earnest	fade	fold
conversation	curl	dig	ease	faint	fond
cook	curse	dinner	educate	false	fool
cool	curtain	dip	efficient	fan	foot
copper	curve	dirt	egg	fancy	forbid
copy	cushion	disappoint	elastic	far	forest
cork	**D**	discipline	elder	farther	forgive
corn	damage	discuss	elect	fat	fork
correct	damp	disgust	electricity	fate	formal
cottage	deaf	dish	elephant	fault	frame
cotton	dear	dismiss	empty	feast	freeze
cough	debt	disturb	empire	feather	frequent
courage	decay	ditch	enclose	female	fresh
cousin	deceive	dive	encourage	fence	fright
cow	decrease	dollar	engine	fever	fruit
coward	deed	donkey	entertain	fierce	fry
crack	deer	dot	envelope	fight	fun

2nd 1,000 words

funeral	guilty	hotel	insure	ladder	loyal
fur	gun	humble	interfere	lake	luck
furnish	**H**	hunger	international	lamp	lump
G	hair	hunt	interrupt	latter	lunch
gallon	hammer	hurry	invent	laugh	lung
gap	handkerchief	hurt	invite	lazy	**M**
garage	harbor	hut	inward	leaf	mad
gas	harm	**I**	island	lean	mail
gay	harvest	instrument	**J**	leather	male
generous	haste	insult	jaw	leg	manage
girl	hat	ice	jealous	lend	manufacture
glory	hate	ideal	jewel	lessen	map
goat	hay	idle	joint	lesson	master
govern	heal	ill	joke	liberty	mat
grace	heap	imagine	journey	lid	match
gradual	heart	imitate	joy	limb	meal
grain	height	immediate	juice	lip	meanwhile
grammar	hesitate	immense	jump	liquid	meat
grand	hinder	important	**K**	list	mechanic
grass	hire	improve	key	literature	medicine
grateful	hit	indoors	kick	load	melt
grave	hole	industry	king	loaf	mend
grease	holiday	inform	kiss	loan	merchant
greed	hollow	ink	kitchen	lock	mercy
greet	holy	in law	knee	lodging	merry
grey	honest	inn	kneel	log	message
grind	hook	inquire	knife	lonely	mild
guess	horizon	insect	knot	loose	milk
guest	hospital	inside	knock	lord	mill
guide	host	instant	**L**	loud	miserable

2nd 1,000 words

mistake	nuisance	patient	pocket	property	recommend
mix	nurse	patriotic	poet	proud	refer
model	nut	pattern	poison	pump	reflect
moderate	**O**	pause	police	punctual	refresh
modest	oar	paw	polish	punish	regret
monkey	obey	pearl	polite	pupil	rejoice
moon	ocean	peculiar	pool	pure	relieve
moral	offend	pen	postpone	purple	remedy
motion	omit	pencil	pot	push	remind
mouse	onto	penny	pour	puzzle	rent
mud	opposite	perform	powder	**Q**	repair
multiply	orange	persuade	practice	qualify	replace
murder	organ	pet	praise	quantity	reproduce
mystery	origin	photograph	pray	quarrel	republic
N	ornament	pick	preach	quart	reputation
nail	overcome	pig	precious	queen	request
neat	**P**	pigeon	prefer	question	rescue
needle	pack	pile	prejudice	quick	reserve
neglect	pad	pin	president	**R**	resign
nephew	pair	pinch	pretend	rabbit	resist
nest	pale	pink	pride	radio	responsible
net	pan	pint	priest	rail	restaurant
nice	parcel	pipe	prison	rain	retire
niece	pardon	pity	prize	rake	revenge
noble	parent	plain	probable	rapid	review
noise	park	plaster	procession	rare	reward
nonsense	particular	plate	profession	rat	ribbon
noon	passage	plenty	profit	raw	rice
nose	paste	plough	prompt	ray	rid
noun	path	plural	pronounce	razor	ripe

2nd 1,000 words

risk	sand	shirt	sorry	stomach	tax
rival	satisfy	shock	soul	stove	taxi
roar	sauce	shop	soup	strap	tea
roast	saucer	shout	sour	straw	telegraph
rob	scatter	shower	sow	strict	telephone
rock	scent	shut	spade	string	temper
rod	scissors	sick	spare	strip	temperature
roof	scold	signal	spell	stripe	temple
root	scorn	silk	spill	stuff	tempt
rope	scrape	sincere	spin	stupid	tend
rot	scratch	sing	spit	suck	tender
row	screen	sink	splendid	sugar	tent
royal	screw	skin	split	suit	thank/s
rub	search	skirt	spoil	supper	theater
rubber	seed	slave	spoon	suspect	think
rubbish	seldom	slide	sport	swallow	thief
rude	sentence	slip	staff	swear	thin
rug	severe	slope	stain	sweat	thirst
ruin	sew	smell	stairs	sweep	thorn
rust	shade	smoke	stamp	swell	thorough
S	shallow	smooth	star	swim	thread
sacred	shame	snake	steady	swing	threaten
sacrifice	sharp	snow	steam	sword	throat
sad	sheep	soap	steep	sympathy	thumb
saddle	sheet	socks	steer	T	thunder
sake	shelf	soldier	stem	tail	ticket
salary	shell	solemn	stiff	tailor	tide
sale	shelter	solid	sting	tall	tidy
salt	shield	solve	stir	tame	tie
sample	ship	sore	stockings	tap	tight

2nd 1,000 words

		U	vessel	weave	worm
till	toy		victory	weed	worry
tin	track	ugly	violent	weigh	worship
tip	translate	umbrella	virtue	wet	wound
tire	trap	uncle	vowel	wheat	wrap
title	tray	unit	voyage	wheel	wreck
tobacco	treasure	unity		whip	wrist
toe	treat	universe	W	whisper	
tomorrow	tremble	upper	wage/s	whistle	Y
ton	trial	upright	waist	whole	yard
tongue	tribe	upset	wake	wicked	yield
tonight	trick	upwards	wander	widow	
tool	trip	urge	warm	wine	Z
tooth	true		wash	wipe	zero
tough	trunk	V	wax	wire	
tour	tube	vain	wealth	witness	
towel	tune	veil	weapon	wool	
tower	twist	verb	weather		
		verse			

82

Acknowledgements

The IELTSedits team acknowledge the following sources of copyright material and are grateful for the permission granted. While every effort has been made, it has not always been possible to identify the sources of all the material used, or to trace all copyright holders. If any omissions are brought to our notice, we will be happy to include the appropriate acknowledgements on reprinting.

The IELTSedits team is especially grateful to the following contributions from New Scientist, Massachusetts Institute of Technology, The National Academies Press, and the School of Linguistics and Applied Language Studies (LALS) at Victoria University of Wellington, New Zealand.

Page 3
https://www.newscientist.com/article/dn27869-animal-brains-connected-up-to-make-mind-melded-computer/

Page 4
https://www.newscientist.com/article/dn27877-burst-of-light-speeds-up-healing-by-turbocharging-our-cells/

Page 5
https://www.newscientist.com/article/dn27851-spy-tech-firm-breach-exposes-extent-of-world-surveillance-market/

Page 6
https://www.newscientist.com/article/dn27836-winning-formula-reveals-if-your-team-is-too-far-ahead-to-lose/

Final Review - pages 65 - 68

Task 1
https://www.newscientist.com/article/dn27115-new-memories-implanted-in-mice-while-they-sleep/

Task 2
https://www.newscientist.com/article/mg22429944-000-ghost-universes-kill-schrodingers-quantum-cat/

Task 3
https://www.newscientist.com/article/mg22429934-000-brain-decoder-can-eavesdrop-on-your-inner-voice/

Task 4
https://www.newscientist.com/article/mg22329842-400-and-now-the-weather-featuring-climate-change-blame/

Task 5
http://entrepreneurship.mit.edu/sites/default/files/documents/
ExecSummary_Entrepreneurial_Impact_The_Role_of_MIT.pdf

Task 6
http://www.nap.edu/openbook.php?record_id=6482&page=7

Printed in July 2021
by Rotomail Italia S.p.A., Vignate (MI) - Italy